Taste of

ISRAEL

A MEDITERRANEAN
FEAST

Taste of
ISRAEL

A MEDITERRANEAN FEAST

✦

AVI GANOR
RON MAIBERG

with Zachi Bukshester and Kenneth R Windsor

M&S

Published in Canada in 1990 by

McClelland & Stewart Inc., *The Canadian Publishers*, 481 University Avenue, Toronto, Ontario M5G 2E9

This book was designed and produced in the United Kingdom by Multimedia Books Limited, 32-34 Gordon House Road, London NW5 1LP

Text © Ron Maiberg 1990   Photography © Avi Ganor 1990
Compilation © Multimedia Books Limited 1990

Photography & Art Direction   *Avi Ganor*
Text & Recipes   *Ron Maiberg*
Design   *Kenneth R Windsor, Metamark International*
Food Stylist & Consultant   *Zachi Bukshester*
Production   *Arnon Orbach*
Research   *Stella Korin-Liber*
Project Coordination   *Sarah Elergant*
Ceramics   *Dafna Botzer*

ISBN 0-7710-6695-3

Printed in Hong Kong by Imago

PHOTOGRAPHS, PAGES 1-8

1. Jaffa oranges, Israel's ambassadors of goodwill. In the background a stretch of seascape in Jaffa.

2. Onion fields in the Golan. Abundance from a fertile land.

3. Labaneh cheese balls in olive oil. Stored in olive oil, labaneh keeps for a long time.

4. Granite mountains in the Judean desert.

5. A colorful display of summer and winter squash.

6. Almond trees in full bloom in Central Galilee.

7. Traditional preparation of zhoug, a fiery Yemenite relish.

8. Strawberries forever. Each year the season is longer and the strawberries bigger.

Above: Goat's cheese with mint and carrots.

ONTENTS

$\mathscr{I}$NTRODUCTION

When asked to write about

Israeli cuisine, foreign food

critics usually resort to the Israeli break-

fast. It is a subject they can be enthusi-

astic about without compromising their

integrity. In most instances, the setting

for this much admired meal is a kibbutz - the pioneering spirit is somehow a fitting backdrop for it. In a kibbutz, the foreign food critic finds himself caught up in an experience which is at once esthetic and gastronomic. He is impressed with the rich display of creams, cheeses, yogurts and buttermilks, set off by a

lush barrage of vegetables. It is an attractive sight, wholesome and full of vitality. It is hard not to respond to it. This, then, is the archetypal scene that has made breakfast, in the eyes of more than one critic, "Israel's main contribution to world cuisine." While in Israel, recommended one critic, eat once a day. Preferably breakfast. Preferably in a kibbutz.

◆ Lahuhua,

Yemenite

spongy

pancakes.

Most of the food we eat in Israel is not indigenous to the Eastern Mediterranean, but it is Israeli by virtue of the fact that it is grown, prepared and eaten here. However, an educated palate can easily identify the major influences at work in Israeli kitchens. There is the North African or Mahgrebi influence. Jews have lived in North Africa for centuries and few surveys of Moroccan food fail to mention the contribution made by the Jewish population. Other influences come from Eastern Europe, where Jews once flourished and prospered. Israel's Arab population has contributed yet other influences. But Arabs and Jews have not assimilated in Israel. They represent two opposing and sometimes hostile cultures, each with its distinctive flavour.

What is Israeli cuisine? To some Israelis, the question is meaningless. How can one describe something which is neither homogeneous nor coherent? But this attitude completely misses the point. Israeli cuisine is unique and deserving of attention precisely because of the plurality of ethnic and cultural influences that compose it. All of these influences - Moroccan, Yemenite, Russian, Arab, Polish - are equally important and the existence of such a wide

selection of cuisines in such a small country is what makes Israeli food worthy of discussion.

The existence of an Israeli cuisine is much debated in Israel today. The population is just about equally divided into those who believe there is no such thing and

those who believe there is. Giving world-renowned dishes Hebrew names is not Israeli cuisine. Filet mignon with blue cheese under a new name is still filet mignon with blue cheese. But those brave chefs who are slowly teaching us to be proud of what we have achieved claim that they are "Israeli" when they combine avocados, oranges and biblical hyssop. They feel they are breaking new ground with their version of St. Peter's fish with *tahini*.

In fact Israeli cuisine went nouvelle before it had a chance to define itself. Local experts claim, for example, that Israel's main contribution to world cuisine is not breakfast but barbecued *foie gras*. We were the first to expose this expensive and rare delicacy to the rigors of open fire. Since *foie gras* is largely fat, its preparation is classically conservative and careful. If not watched like a hawk, it can easily melt away. Usually it is made into pâté or

◆ *A Yemenite dancer in the robe traditionally worn on festive occasions such as weddings.*

cooked whole and served warm or cold. Grilling goose liver on a spit is therefore either a demonstration of courage or an act of defiance against the order of the old world. And what could be more outrageously Israeli than serving *foie gras* in *pita* bread?

At this particular moment, Israel is in culinary ferment, still assimilating the influx of new cuisines - French, Italian, American - introduced in the early eighties, but beginning to realize that it has its own character. Anomalies abound. We have, for instance, a white desert truffle which is inedible. We have an artichoke named after Jerusalem, which is not an artichoke

◆ Head shot of a carp, Israel's national fish.

and has nothing to do with Jerusalem. Hyssop, an herb mentioned in the Bible, is now a protected plant, so nobody is allowed to pick it. We now raise more lamb than we can eat, so we are having to educate Jews to like chops, roast leg of lamb and lamb fries rather than beef. Until five years ago, we had only sweet red wine and respectable table wines were termed "sour" and shunned.

Our grandmothers did more than most to formulate an Israeli cuisine, although recent influences have obscured their achievement. They cooked according to their respective backgrounds but adapted their creativity to local produce and weather conditions.

My Russian grandmother used to bake a brown and fragrant *cholent*, a substantial casserole of meat and potatoes, beans and barley, in the oven of our family bakery. It was a large commercial oven, built of red bricks, and my grandmother knew to a fraction of a degree when the temperature was right for her *cholent*. She would put it in, covered with a kitchen towel, just after the last Sabbath *challah* loaf was taken out early on Friday morning and let it cook until the next morning. She tended her *cholent* all through the night as if it were a child. Every hour, on the hour, she would wake up, march briskly to the bakery, pull the pot out of the deep oven, remove the towel carefully so as not to wake the *cholent*, and measure the amount of liquid left in the pot. Her nightmare was that her *cholent* would dry up. Having raised three children against terrific odds, she had no intention of this happening.

Nothing that I have ever eaten compares with the *cholent* that

came out of that old blackened pot. Aided by plain water, smartly added, the potatoes turned golden and soft, the beans tied up with the barley, and the meat blended with the bone marrow until it was impossible to tell them apart. It took dedication and stamina, and

my grandmother had both. Even her hand-made eggplant salad remains, to my mind, more typically Israeli than anything we eat today. She burnt the eggplants over an open fire, peeled them, mashed them with a fork, then added garlic, lemon juice, mayonnaise and hot peppers. Her pickles were excellent. Even her simple breakfast omelets were memorable.

My Polish grandmother, who came from Cracow, had standards every bit as tough and rigid as those of my Russian grandmother. She did not fry, and she never used glowing charcoals, let alone grilled over them. She

◆ *Early morning in Safed, an ancient hilltop town famous for its clear air, occasional snow and its devout residents.*

17

used to cook meat with sour cream and capers - strictly non-kosher. Her carp, very sweet and totally inedible to the modern Israeli palate, used to quiver in a molded prison of jelly. Her cucumber salad with fresh dill and cream was very good, though. She also in-first artichoke, which and exciting as my showed me how to leaves and nibble the end, and how to pluck down, and how to slice each tasty morsel in expert on sauces, but

troduced me to my was almost as erotic first girlfriend. She remove the outer flesh from the stem away the thistle-the heart and dip white sauce. I am no I can improvise a sauce for artichokes based on what I remember of my grandmother's. She also bought us our first whole goose liver, a round and massive ball wrapped in foil, and taught us how to eat it. That was in the early sixties, when *foie gras* was as foreign as lobster and pheasant, both by the way still unavailable. Unlike my Russian grandmother, who was an extrovert, my Polish grandmother never ate at the table. She never really served either, in the sense of dispensing food to others. She shoved food in front of us and commanded us to eat. She would not relax until everything was finished and was furious if something was left untouched. I always hoped, for her sake, that she sneaked something in the kitchen, but people who knew her better told me not to count on it.

The world's great cuisines were formed during lengthy periods of peace and fun. One might almost say that stability and parties are prerequisites for true gastronomy. Such prerequisites have seldom been the lot of Jews or Israelis. We have scarcely had time for leisure, no time to play enjoyable games, and the dietary laws of *kashrut* have discouraged us from mixing meat with milk and eating seafood. So, all things considered, it is a wonder that so many tasty things have emerged from the Israeli kitchen. In the early years we had to make do with very little. Now we have found our culinary voice. It is high time that it was heard.

◆ *At the end of a day of harvest, bales of hay await collection in the Jezreel Valley.*

Taste of
ISRAEL

A MEDITERRANEAN
FEAST

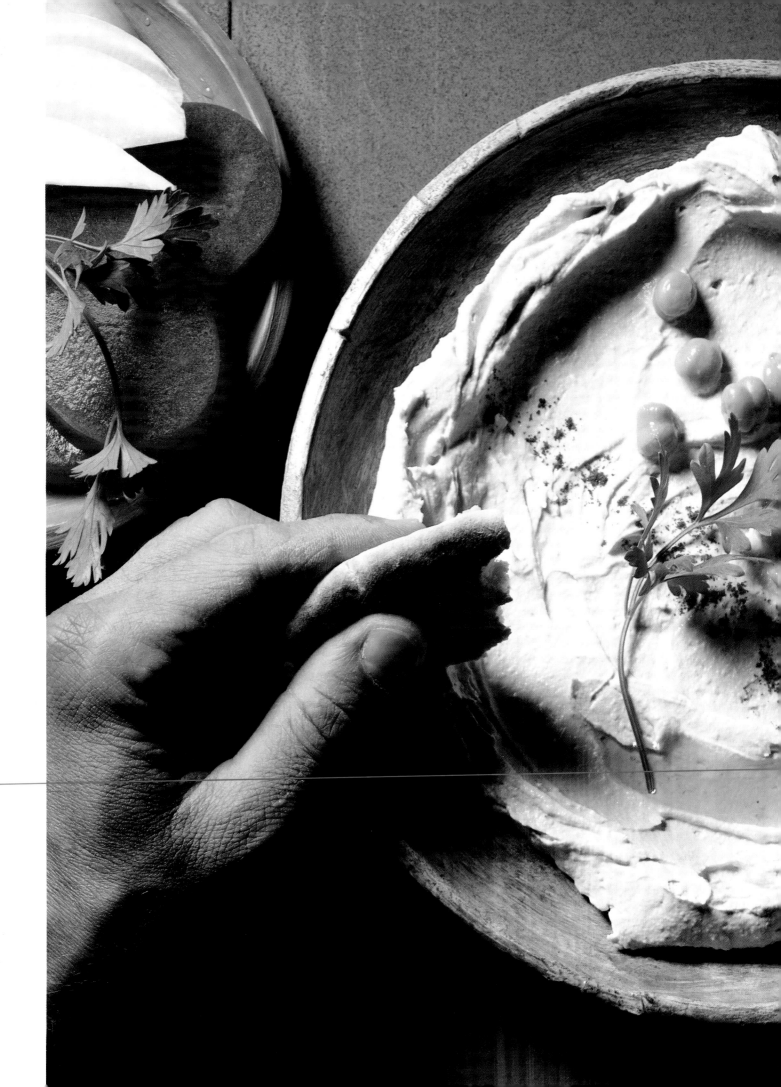

STARTERS &
HOT STUFF

◆ Hummus, *an aerial*
view. One of Israel's
national foods, hummus
is filling, nutrititious
and cheap. No knives or
forks are needed, just
pita *bread and an*
expert wrist. In view:
whole chickpeas, olive oil,
paprika, parsley, pickled
turnips and raw onion
for added pungency.

Mezze can be translated

as appetizers, starters,

hors d'oeuvres, snacks. But none of

these words conveys the range of

delicacies, cooked and uncooked,

which constitute the start of a meal in

◆ *A eucalyptus tree in sand dunes near Nitzana, on the desert borders of the northern Negev.*

Israel and throughout the Middle East.

Although going to restaurants is not always the best way to learn about or judge the food of a country, in the case of *mezze* I thoroughly recommend it. You will encounter, in one sitting, an enormous variety of dishes, far more than any single household can muster. Even a modest restaurant runs to at least twenty different items.

The portions are small, but they are an ideal introduction to the exotic and unfamiliar. There are crudités, served with various dips, *hummus*, *tahini*, lemony *labaneh* cheese, cheese in cubes, grilled chicken livers, eggplants prepared in a variety of ways, salads laced with turmeric and cumin, pickled vegetables, fried *kibbeh* or meat patties, stuffed vine leaves, small pastries filled with meat or cheese or spinach, and fiery relishes such as *harissa* and *zhoug*. In fact any dish can be considered part of the *mezze* table if it has a strong individual taste and comes in small portions.

This diversity reveals something else about Israeli food. We shy away from eating our meals as set courses served in sequence, with each course calculated to feed a given number of people. We like to spread our food out on the table so that we can help ourselves. Although variety is the spice of life, an indiscriminate jumble of *mezze* piled on the same plate is frowned upon. One is supposed to pick and choose rather than eat everything in sight, simultaneously.

The fiery concoctions served with *mezze* are as invigorating as they look. *Zhoug, shatta, hreimeh, harissa* and *madbuha* are all based in varying degrees on green and red chili peppers, all locally grown. Fresh horseradish is tame by comparison. Chili-based relishes are a staple of Israeli food. No meal is complete without them. At most restaurants you do not have to ask for them. They are always on the table. They perk up any and every *mezze*, can be blended with *hummus* and *tahini*, squirted over *falafel*, and added to casseroles and grilled meats. They cross ethnic barriers with the same ease as the aroma of baking bread, and even if they were once the prerogative of Yemenite and Moroccan immigrants, they are now consumed by all and considered common property. To the novice diner, they are dangerous and part of a game Israelis love to play on the unwary. Beware of Israelis bearing hot peppers.

◆ *Sunset over the Judean desert.*

　　　　Yemenite Jews claim that *zhoug* and *shatta*, two of the most explosive of these condiments, have the power to ward off all sorts of diseases, from the common cold to blocked coronary arteries. There have even been scientific studies that tried to establish cause and effect between hot food and rude health, but they were inconclusive. The ability of various communities to eat *harissa* and its relatives without flinching is an indication of health in itself.

　　　　On the face of it, the appeal of the red hot chili pepper is hard to reconcile with the agony it causes. The taste is difficult to describe, for it is not so much a taste as a sensation of great heat applied to a small area. It is wise to have *pita* or some other bread within reach, bread being the only food that seems to soothe chili burns.

　　　　The truth is that chili paste is a macho game even deadlier than poker. You never let on when you're down. You never admit that your

◆ *Traditional*
preparation of
Yemenite
zhoug. Hot
peppers and
garlic are
crushed and
ground by
hand, then
mixed with
coriander and
spices.

mucous membranes hurt like hell. A man's suffering can only be judged by the sweat on his brow. He never makes a dash for the restroom to stick his head in a sink of cold water. He keeps scooping until the last fragment of *pita* is finished.

Commercially grown chili peppers are regarded, by purists, as lacking in virtue. They lose some of their potency during transport and handling, they say. They would rather pluck the peppers that grow in their grandmother's garden than spend money on store-bought peppers.

Chili peppers are shrouded in folklore. Small jars of home-made chili paste are sold in local markets and those which have an old, old woman standing behind them are thought to have extra potency and

◆ *A typical Israeli chili pepper. There are only a few kinds and this is the most common.*

authenticity. In the old Yemenite quarter of Tel Aviv, *zhoug* and *shatta* are still prepared by hand. The preparation is quite simple, but one has to wear gloves and protect the eyes and other sensitive areas. Fresh, crisp chili peppers are ground by hand on a large flat stone, or chopped up and pounded on a stone mortar, then mixed with spices and herbs. Stored in jars with tightly fitting lids, the mixture keeps for months.

Other Jewish communities have their own hot and not so hot stuffs. Moroccans use *harissa* and *hermulla*, also based on chili peppers and mixed with salt and garlic. Rumanians like to use freshly minced garlic, mixed with vinegar and other liquids, on their meat, serving it like any other condiment.

Chili peppers are second nature to many Israelis, and eaten with all meals, even with breakfast. Bitter comments are made if they are not hot and fiery enough. Regretfully, there are seasons when they are less potent.

$\mathscr{S}$TARTERS &

HOT STUFF

◆ *A selection*

of mezze,

the traditonal

Israeli and

Middle

Eastern

starters.

$\mathscr{R}ecipes$

STUFFED GRAPE LEAVES

8 oz/225g fresh or preserved grape/vine leaves
1 1/3 cups/250g long-grain rice
2 or 3 tomatoes, skinned and chopped
1 large onion, finely chopped
2 tablespoons finely chopped fresh parsley
1 tablespoon dried crushed mint
1/4 teaspoon ground cinnamon
1/2 teaspoon ground allspice
salt and freshly ground black pepper
2 tomatoes, sliced (optional)
1/2 cup/100ml olive oil
1/4 teaspoon powdered saffron (optional)
1 teaspoon sugar
juice of 1 lemon
lemon wedges, to garnish

If you are using grape leaves preserved in brine, the excess salt must be removed. Put them into a large bowl and pour boiling water over them, making sure the water penetrates between the layers. Let the leaves soak for 20 minutes, then drain them and soak them in fresh cold water. Drain and repeat the process.

If you are using fresh grape leaves, soften them by plunging them into boiling water for a few minutes, then shave off the harder part of the stem.

Wash the rice, soak it for 10 minutes, then drain it. Add boiling water, stir the rice around, then drain it and rinse under cold running water.

Mix the rice with the chopped tomatoes, onion, parsley, mint, spices, salt and pepper. Place a generous spoonful of this mixture near the stem end of each grape leaf. Fold the stem end over the stuffing, fold both sides towards the middle, then roll up the package like a small cigar. Squeeze lightly in the palm of your hand. The process gets easier once you have rolled a few!

Pack the stuffed leaves tightly in a large, shallow pan lined with sliced tomatoes and any torn or imperfect grape leaves. Add a clove of garlic here and there if you like.

Mix the olive oil with the water, saffron (if used), sugar and lemon juice, and pour it over the stuffed leaves. Put a plate on top of the leaves to prevent them unwinding, cover the pan, and simmer very, very gently for at least 2 hours, adding water from time to time as the liquid in the pan is absorbed. Leave the stuffed leaves in the pan to cool. Serve cold with lots of lemon wedges.
Serves 5 or 6

TABBOULEH
A salad of cracked wheat, vegetables & herbs

1 cup bulgur/cracked wheat
4 tablespoons chopped fresh flat-leaved parsley
2 tablespoons chopped mint
1 cucumber, diced
1 bell pepper
1 onion/6 scallions, diced
1 large tomato, diced
grated rind of 1 lemon
juice of 2 lemons
1/3 cup/80 ml olive oil
salt and pepper
pinch ground allspice

Soak the bulgur/cracked wheat in cold water for 30 minutes, then drain in a fine sieve, squeezing out the excess moisture. In a salad bowl, combine all ingredients.

Serve as a tangy starter, but not before refrigerating for 1 hour.

◆ *Stuffed grape leaves*

are eaten in most

Eastern Mediterranean countries,

nean countries,

including Greece,

Turkey, Lebanon

and Cyprus.

The filling can be

rice or meat or

both.

TAHINI SAUCE

A savoury sauce based on sesame seeds

1/2 cup/100g sesame paste
1/4 cup/60ml water
1/4 cup/60ml fresh lemon juice
1/4 teaspoon salt
1 teaspoon finely minced garlic

Using a fork, blend together the sesame paste and water, then add the lemon juice, parsley and garlic, mixing well after each addition. Alternatively, mix all the ingredients together in a blender. The mixture will thicken later in the refrigerator.

A *mezze* version of *tahini* sauce calls for lots of fresh, finely chopped coriander or parsley as well. Keeps in the refrigerator for up to 10 days.

CUCUMBER AND FENNEL SALAD

1 large cucumber, peeled and finely chopped
1/4 bulb fennel, finely chopped
pinch of salt
1/4 teaspoon freshly ground black pepper
3 tablespoons sour cream
1 tablespoon olive oil
2 tablespoons fresh lemon juice
2 scallions/spring onions, finely chopped

Thoroughly combine all the ingredients, and chill well before serving. Serves 4.

EGGPLANT SALAD

Three versions out of many

1 lb/450g eggplants/aubergines

5 tablespoons fresh lemon juice
scant teaspoon minced garlic
1 teaspoon salt
or
1/2 cup/100ml tahini sauce
(see recipe opposite)
coarsely chopped parsley, to garnish
or
1/2 cup mayonnaise
2 tablespoons chopped onion
1 tablespoon diced red pepper
2 tablespoons olive oil
1 tablespoon chopped dill

Prick the eggplants a few times with a fork, then bake over charcoal until the skins are blistered and black. This is usually done after grilling meat, while the barbecue is still hot. Otherwise it can be done under the broiler/grill, or in the oven, but the smoky aroma will be missing. Allow the eggplants to cool, then remove the skins. Mash the flesh in a food processor (connoisseurs never use anything but a fork!), then stir in one of the three flavorings listed above. Serve cold, with hot *pita* bread.

JELLIED CALF'S FOOT

3 - 4 lbs/1.4-1.9kg calf's feet
10 cups/2.0 liters water
6 cloves garlic
1 carrot
2 medium size onions
1 celery
fresh thyme
4 bay leaves
salt and black pepper to taste
2 hard-boiled eggs, sliced
lemon wedges, to garnish

Blanch the calf's feet (plunge them into boiling water, bring the water to a boil again, then remove the feet and wash them). Cut each one into 3 or 4 pieces, put the pieces into a sauce-pan with the 10 cups/2 liters of water, then bring to a boil and skim. Add all the other ingredients, except for the eggs, and simmer until the slices of calf's foot are tender - this takes about 4 hours.

Strain the broth, taste it, and add salt and pepper to taste. At this stage some cooks clarify the broth as for consommé, using egg whites and egg shells. Pick the celery, bay leaves, thyme and bones out of the strainer - this should be done by hand, even though the contents of the strainer are very sticky. Grind/mince whatever is left in the strainer and return it to the broth.

To see whether the broth will gel or not, put a spoonful on a plate and put the plate in the freezer for 10 minutes. If necessary, add 1/2 oz/15g unflavored gelatin to the broth.

Arrange the slices of hard-boiled egg in a shallow dish, ladle the broth over them, and put the dish in the refrigerator for several hours.

When ready to serve, cut the jelly into 8 portions, transfer it to a serving plate and garnish with lemon wedges.

◆ *Jellied calf's foot is a traditional Jewish dish from Eastern Europe. It is eaten with generous helpings of lemon juice.*

◆ *Moroccan*

cigars are rolled

sheets of filo

dough, deep-

fried, with

different

fillings. They

are a favorite on

festive

occasions.

MOROCCAN CIGARS

In Israel *filo* dough is often made into filled "cigars." Several variations on the theme are given below. The fillings are spread on half-leaves of *filo*, then the edges of the *filo* are folded over and the dough is rolled up into a cigar shape. The edges are sealed with egg white or with a mixture of flour and water. The cigars are then fried in deep oil for 2 minutes until they turn golden. Plan on 6-8 cigars per person as a starter.

FILLING FOR MEAT CIGARS
1 onion, chopped
1 tablespoon oil
6 oz/180g ground/minced meat
1 teaspoon chopped parsley
1/4 teaspoon ground cumin
pinch of cinnamon
salt and pepper to taste

Fry the onion in the oil, then add the meat, parsley, spices and seasoning. For a real treat, add a little finely chopped goose liver too.

FILLING FOR POTATO CIGARS
1 onion, chopped
1 tablespoon vegetable oil
5 oz/150g boiled potatoes, mashed
salt, white pepper and nutmeg to taste

Fry the onions in the oil, then mix well with the mashed potato and seasoning.

FILLING FOR CHEESE CIGARS
4 oz/125g cheese, grated
fresh mint leaves

Put two leaves of mint into each cigar before you roll it up.

CHOPPED LIVER

1 cup/225ml oil
2 large onions, sliced
1 lb/450g chicken livers
5 or 6 hard-boiled eggs
salt and pepper
radishes and tomato slices, to garnish

Heat the oil and fry the onions until they are golden brown, then drain them on paper towels/kitchen paper. Set aside 1/4 cup/60ml of the oil and fry the chicken livers in the rest. Drain the livers on paper towels and allow them to cool. Discard the oil in which they were cooked.

Grind/mince the chicken livers, the fried onions and the hard-boiled eggs, then mix them all together, adding pepper and salt to taste. Slowly blend in the reserved oil until the mixture is the consistency of a smooth spread. Serve garnished with radishes and slices of tomato. Chopped liver is traditionally eaten with a fork or spread onto a slice of *challah* (see recipe p. 90).

◆ *Chopped liver,*

pickles, and

beer at a

Levinsky

Street diner

in Tel Aviv.

◆ *One of the*

wonders of

Jewish cuisine -

chopped liver,

on toasted

challah.

MOROCCAN CARROT SALAD

1 1/2 lbs/700g carrots
1 bulb garlic, finely chopped
1/2 cup/100ml vegetable oil
1 tablespoon finely chopped chili peppers
1 teaspoon sweet paprika
3/4 cup/180ml water
salt
ground turmeric
1/3 cup/80ml vinegar
1 tablespoon lemon juice
1 tablespoon chopped parsley

Wash and peel the carrots, and boil or steam them until they are tender but still firm. Drain them and allow to cool. Gently fry the garlic in the oil until it is soft and transparent - this takes about 12 minutes. Now add the chili peppers and paprika to the pan and fry for 1 minute. Pour in the water, then add the cooked carrots, salt, turmeric, vinegar and lemon juice. Simmer for 5 minutes, then remove from the heat, allow to cool, cover, and refrigerate for 24 hours. Stir well before serving, sprinkled with parsley. Serve as cold starter or to accompany *couscous* (see photograph p. 108).

◆ *Chicken*

livers,

egg, onion,

and a

meat grinder

spell...chopped

liver.

ONIONS WITH VINEGAR

2 large mild/Spanish onions
salt
2 or 3 tablespoons white wine vinegar
1 tablespoon dried mint or
chopped fresh parsley

Peel and slice the onions into half rings and sprinkle them with a little salt. Combine them with the vinegar and mint, and allow to stand for at least 1 hour before serving. They will become soft, lose much of their pungency, and absorb the other flavors. Serve them as an appetizer or as a relish with a main dish.

PICKLED TURNIPS

2 lbs/450g turnips
1 raw beet/beetroot
juice of 1/2 lemon
1 1/2 heaped tablespoons salt
6 cups/1.4 liters water

Wash the turnips and the beet, but do not peel them. Cut both into slices 1/4 inch/ 0.5cm thick. Sprinkle the slices of beet with the lemon juice and lay them in the bottom of a squat glass jar (they will give the turnips a reddish tinge). Now pack the turnip slices on top and add salted water to cover. Seal and keep in a cool place for 7 days. Serve with other *mezze* dishes.

◆ *Some people*

pickle everything

- turnips,

carrots,

cucumbers, red

peppers, whole

lemons, olives,

garlic...

HOT OLIVE SALAD

1 lb/450g green olives, pitted
2 large ripe tomatoes, skinned and grated
1/3 cup/80ml vegetable oil
6 cloves garlic, crushed
1 tablespoon tomato paste/purée
3 slices unpeeled lemon
1 teaspoon chili powder
1 teaspoon red pepper
salt and freshly ground black pepper

Put the olives into a saucepan, cover them with water, and bring to a boil. Drain, cover with water again, and repeat the process. In another saucepan, mix the tomatoes with the oil, garlic and tomato paste, and simmer together for a few minutes. Now add the olives, lemon slices, spices, salt and pepper, and mix well together. Add a little water and simmer over a low heat until the water is absorbed. Remove the lemon and set aside to cool. Serve cold as a *mezze* dish.

◆ *A feast of olives: cracked olives, and hot red peppers.*

ZHOUG
Chili paste with parsley and coriander

1 cup/225g puréed fresh chili peppers,
green or red
8 tablespoons chopped fresh parsley
8 tablespoons chopped fresh coriander
1 1/2 tablespoons minced garlic
1 teaspoon salt
1 teapoon pepper
1 teaspoon ground cumin
pinch of ground cardamom

Use a food processor to purée the chili peppers. Then add the parsley and coriander and blend again. Add the garlic, salt, pepper, cumin, and cardamom.

Re-blend, spoon into a glass jar, seal, and refrigerate. *Zhoug* will keep for several months in the refrigerator.

The red version uses *only* red chili peppers and no herbs and though more common it lacks the typical Yemenite flavor of the green version.

Zhoug is served with Yemenite dishes such as *chilbe* or *mlawach*, with a small bowl of freshly puréed tomatoes.

HUMMUS
Chickpea dip with garlic and *tahini*

1 1/2 cups/350g dry chickpeas
1 teaspoon baking soda
3 or 4 cloves garlic, minced
1 teaspoon salt
1/2 teaspoon ground cumin
1/2 cup/100ml tahini sauce (see p. 30)
juice of 2 lemons
olive oil

Soak the chickpeas in water overnight, with the soda. Cook them until soft, then drain them, reserving a little of the cooking liquid. Reserve a few whole chickpeas for garnishing.

Mash all the ingredients together, but not too finely. If the consistency is too dry, add a little of the chickpea cooking liquid. Spoon the mixture onto a plate and make a well in the center. A skilled hummus artist can make a perfect crater with a thin film of paste in the middle in one swift, circular movement. Put a little olive oil, and the reserved chickpeas, into the well and serve. Some cooks like to add extra *tahini*.

◆ *The twin towers of Yemenite cuisine: green zhoug and red zhoug, two fiery condiments which are chiefly responsible for the flavor of Yemenite food.*

◆ *The Dead Sea is the lowest place on earth. It is rich with minerals and phosphates, and nothing ever grows in it.*

HAZERET/HREIN
Horseradish relish

3 oz/100g fresh horseradish
10 oz/275g fresh beets/beetroot
1/2 cup/100ml vinegar
1 teaspoon salt
2 tablespoons sugar

Peel the horseradish. Wash the beets, then boil them for 15 minutes. When cool, peel them. Now grate the horseradish and the beets using a fine grater or a food processors - do this near an open window! Mix the grated horseradish and beets with the other ingredients and refrigerate in a glass jar. Use as a condiment with any traditional Eastern European savoury dish, and never ever attempt to serve gefilte fish without it.

HARISSA
A North African condiment

18 fresh red chili peppers
2 red bell peppers
4 cloves garlic
1 teaspoon ground cumin
1 teaspoon coriander seeds
1/2 teaspoon hot chili powder
1 teaspoon coarse salt
3 tablespoons white vinegar
2 tablespoons olive oil

Remove the stalks and seeds from the chili peppers - make sure you wear gloves to do this. Using a pestle and mortar (or a food processor, which is less fun), grind the peppers up with the garlic and spices. Deseed the bell peppers and deep-fry or broil/grill them; remove the skins. Add the flesh to the chili paste, with the rest of the ingredients, and grind for another minute or two. Keep a week's supply in the refrigerator and freeze the rest.

HREIMEH
Spicy Moroccan fish

3 tablespoons vegetable oil
2 tablespoons chopped parsley
1 onion, chopped
8 cloves garlic, chopped
2 tablespoons tomato paste/purée
1/2 teaspoon salt
2 tablespoons lemon juice
1/4 teaspoon black pepper
ground coriander or cumin, to taste
1/2 teaspoon paprika
1 1/2 cups/350ml water
1 lb/450g fresh fish (sea bass, gray mullet or carp)

In a saucepan, heat the oil and fry the onion and parsley for 5 minutes. Add the garlic, tomato paste, salt, lemon juice, black pepper and coriander or cumin. Add the water, mix well, and cook for 5-10 minutes over a medium heat.

Lay the fish in the saucepan, cover, and poach in the spicy broth for 25 minutes.

◆ *Horseradish sauce, flavored with beets, is the sole hot contribution to Israeli cuisine by Eastern European Jews. A customary condiment of Passover, it is eaten as a reminder of a harsh and bitter past.*

DAIRY & CHEESE

◆ *Shultza, the*
shepherd, tends
his flock of
goats in the
northern region
of the country.
The milk is
used to make
rich, fatty
cheese.

In Byniamina, along a narrow passageway called Cypress Road, in the back room of Shomron Dairy, a shop as fragrant as its name is musical, Moshe Bachar cuts into a burnished-brown wheel of Turkish *kachkavel* with

a small knife shaped like a spade. Using the knife as a wedge, he cracks open the huge, damp, moldy cheese into two craggy halves, then bends down and squints at its texture.

"Horef" he says. "Winter."

Abu-Mussa, an Arab who makes his living tapping the sides of thousands of wheels of *kachkavel* each year, nods in agreement. He taps the cheeses with a tiny steel hammer, listening carefully for evidence of unwanted holes in their moist interior. "Too white, not yellow straw," he comments, referring to the color the cheese should have been if the goats that provided the milk for it had eaten the deep green grass and alfalfa of summer.

Moshe Bachar is a third-generation cheese-maker and a native-born Israeli. The huge 45-lb/20-kg wheel of 1988 vintage cheese has been made from the milk of goats fed on winter fodder. It is a winter cheese, too white, too young, a bit too acid to eat as a dessert with red wine. But it will be a wonderful cheese for cooking with vegetables, perfect for grating over pasta.

A 1987 vintage wheel, a rare cheese to have since demand is such that Bachar cannot allow his cheeses to age properly and gracefully, is described as "a little elder sister." It is tinged with yellow inside, and its texture is more moist, a sign that it possesses more style and breeding. It was made from the milk of spring. Bachar forgets his dismay over the young and restless *kachkavel* and takes a bite of its elder sister. It deserves its appellation. Just look at its golden color and the ragged veins running through it like a mother lode! "Like silk," Bachar breathes.

◆ *Shultza tending his flock near a water hole.*

◆ *For a fixed price, the Ein Kamonim roadside inn, in the Upper Galilee offers a tray of assorted cheeses, country-style bread, vegetables, homemade wine, pickles, vinegar, and olive oil. Fire crackles in the fireplace in winter.*

◆ *Fresh ricotta*

cheese in cheese-

cloth, still

dripping whey,

Shomron Dairy,

Byniamina.

Kachkavel, also known as *kasseri*, is an aristocratic cheese, the people of Byniamina say, the king of cheeses, made by hand and with love, just as it has been for a hundred years. It is also produced in a few villages on the

Golan Heights, Druze villages that have never stopped making it. Their *kachkavel* is stronger and sharper than Bachar's. Byniamina's citizens boast of the strawberries, oranges and zucchini that grow in the rich fields around their city, but most of all they revel in their cheese. Goats are imported and bred specially for the richness and quantity of their milk, the milk that will become *kachkavel*. Cheese-making in Byniamina is considered a high calling, an art not taught in any other way than by father to son, mother to daughter. The whey that is the by-product of the cheese-making process becomes food for Byniamina's cows and Byniamina swears that its beef is wonderful only because the milk of its goats is so rich.

Before the cheese-making process begins, two collections of milk are needed, and these must be blended carefully. Cheese-making begins at about five o'clock each morning and ends at about noon, "and it must be done three hundred and sixty-five days a year" Bachar explains "because goats do not know about holy days."

The evening's milk is brought in, poured into shallow stainless steel tanks, and left overnight. It separates into two components, heavy cream that sinks to the bottom and lighter skim milk. The next morning the skim milk,

◆ *Dairy produce being delivered in the early morning hours from the back of a truck, Tel Aviv.*

containing virtually no fat, is drained from the tanks and mixed in copper cooking kettles with that morning's collection of fresh, whole milk. Combining the two milks is an arduous business. The copper kettles hold 240 gallons/1,100 liters each and although the milks can be and are mixed by giant beaters, the cheese-makers insist on mixing them partly by hand. They like to feel and touch the milk. "It is our way of making the cheese ours" says Bachar.

A portion of the whey from the previous day is added to the milk mixture and the heat is turned on under the kettles. The whey, Bachar explains, is rich in lactic acid, the perfect ingredient for beginning the ripening process. As the milk is heated to 95°F/35°C, Abu-Mussa keeps reaching for and reading the temperature on a special thermometer immersed in the milk. When the correct temperature is reached, he turns off the heat and adds a bit of rennet to each kettle. Rennet, from the stomachs of calves, will curdle the milk.

And so the process goes on, fresh milk at one end and ripened cheese at the other. But not so long ago, when Bachar's cheese had a chance to age gracefully, most Israelis subsisted on fresh white cheese. It was the only kind made. It was never aged and had no taste or aroma to speak of. It was spread on bread or used in cakes and cooking. It contained 5-9 percent fat and freshness was all. The only milk product with a hint of maturity to it was *labaneh*, made from curdled yogurt, and that was an Arab invention. *Labaneh*, a thick

◆ *Cows grazing in lush winter pasture, Byniamina.*

lemony paste traditionally stored in glass jars filled with olive oil, keeps for a long time without refrigeration. No one grated cheese - there was no cheese worth grating - and no one served cheese as a separate course.

As with other aspects of Israeli food and cooking, it was foreign travel that brought about a change of taste. New demand created new products. Matured cheese has been with us for ten years or so now, but blue-veined cheese, of which we have only one variety, is still viewed with suspicion unless it is disguised in a dip. We are past wine-and-cheese get-togethers as a means of introducing new cheeses, but only just. We have still not assimilated the culinary possibilities of cheese. Of course the Jewish dietary laws forbid the mixing of milk products and meat, so cooking meat with butter or cream is out

of the question. This is one of the reasons why Israeli cuisine makes such limited use of dairy products in cooking. Margarine is substituted for butter and ersatz cream for the real thing.

Even in this age of refrigerators and well stocked supermarkets, a disappointing number of "new" offerings are really old products under new names. Many varieties of cream cheese are sold which are not really cheese at all, but dips which start off as white cheese which is then mixed with various flavorings and colorings. Fortunately, however, not everyone is content with pseudo cheese. There are farms with small dairy herds and flocks which choose to produce the real thing and we now have a reasonable, although limited, range of bries, chèvres and cheddars, and even a little ricotta and mozarella. These are still a far cry from the great originals, but they hold their own. If you sample them in their own right, and do not make too many comparisons, they are acceptable.

◆ *Stacks of* kachkavel *wheels drying in Shomron Dairy. The hard yellow cheese is also known as* kasseri.

$\mathcal{D}$ AIRY
$\mathscr{O}$ CHEESE

◆ *If it's* labaneh,
it must be
breakfast.
Labaneh *in*
olive oil with
za'atar *and*
scallions, is
morning fare.

$\mathscr{R}ecipes$

GRILLED PEPPERS WITH YOGURT

3 red bell peppers, halved lengthwise and cored
7 oz/200g pecans, shelled and halved
vegetable oil
2 1/2 cups/600ml thick plain yogurt
2 teaspoons salt

Lightly brush the peppers with vegetable oil and cook them under a pre-heated broiler/ grill until soft. Fry the pecans in a little oil until golden, then drain on paper towels/ kitchen paper. Stir the salt into the yogurt.

For a hearty Sephardic breakfast, lay the peppers on top of the yogurt and top with nuts and a sprinkling of mint. Serves 4.

CHILLED CUCUMBER & YOGURT SOUP

1 large cucumber
salt
2 1/2 cups/600ml plain yogurt
1/2 cup/100ml fresh tomato paste/purée
1 clove garlic, chopped very fine
pinch ground coriander
chopped fresh mint and paprika, to garnish

Wash the cucumber, but do not peel it. Chop it coarsely, sprinkle it with salt, and set aside for 30 minutes - this removes some of the bitter taste. Rinse and drain the cucumber, put it in the food processor with the rest of the ingredients, and blend until smooth and creamy.

Serve well chilled, sprinkled with mint and paprika. Serves 4.

◆ *Red peppers roasted on an open fire, with yogurt, chopped mint and pecan nuts.*

CHEESE BLINTZES
Cheese-filled pancakes

BATTER
1 cup/100g all-purpose/plain flour
1 tablespoon sugar
1/4 teaspoon salt
1 cup/225ml milk
4 large eggs, lightly beaten
1 teaspoon unsalted butter, softened or melted
2 tablespoons/40g extra butter for frying

CHEESE FILLING
1 1/2 cups/350g cottage cheese
2 cups/450g cream cheese, softened
2 large egg yolks
3/4 cup/175g sugar
1/2 teaspoon salt
1/2 teaspoon vanilla extract/essence
1 teaspoon grated lemon peel
1/4 cup/60g unsalted butter

2 cups/450ml sour cream
3 cups/500g strawberries

In a blender, mix all the batter ingredients to a smooth consistency and chill for 10 minutes.

Lightly butter a small non-stick skillet/ frying pan and heat it thoroughly. Pour 2 tablespoons of batter into it, tilting the pan so that the batter forms a thin, even layer.

As soon as the batter has solidified, re-move the skillet from the heat, flip the blintz over using a spatula and slide it onto a warm dish. Repeat until all the batter is used up.

Beat together the filling ingredients. Fill each blintz with 2 tablespoons of filling, fold the sides over the filling and roll up. To serve, fry 2 blintzes per person for 2 min-utes on each side, seam-side down first. Serve with sour cream and strawberries. To be polite, offer sifted confectioner's/ icing sugar too.

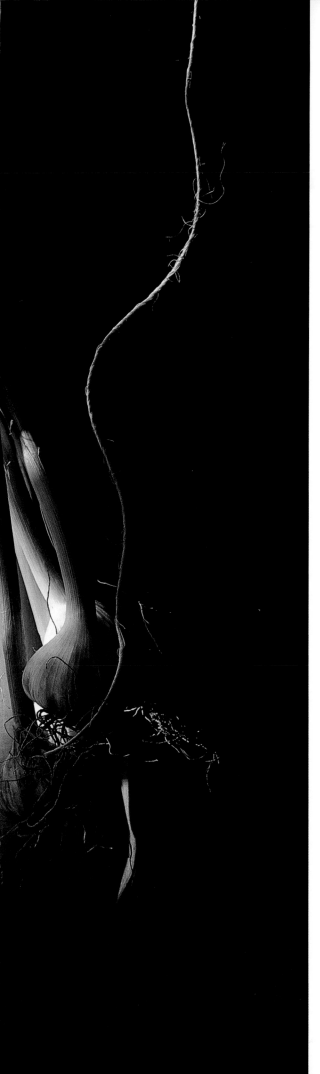

◆ *A household*

staple: labaneh

cheese balls in

olive oil, with

rosemary and

chili peppers.

LABANEH CHEESE BALLS

2 teaspoons salt
2 pints/1 liter plain sheep's milk yogurt
olive oil
coarsely ground black pepper
crushed dried mint or paprika

Mix the salt and yogurt together, then tie it in fine cheesecloth/muslin, and leave it to drain over a bowl or sink for 48 hours. This gets rid of the excess moisture. (In this form it can be eaten spread on bread, with a little chopped fresh mint or wild thyme, or used to make the salad below.)

Chill the cheese in the refrigerator, then roll it into balls about the size of plums and store in olive oil with a sprig of rosemary and 1-2 dried chili peppers. When you want to eat them, remove them from the oil, drain, and roll in pepper and mint/paprika.

LABANEH & CUCUMBER SALAD

8 oz/225g labaneh *cheese*
(see recipe above)
2 tablespoons milk
4 baby cucumbers, unpeeled and finely diced
2 cloves garlic, crushed
1 teaspoon dried mint
salt
1 tablespoon olive oil

Mash the cheese to a smooth paste with the milk, then add the cucumber, garlic, mint and salt, and mix well. Add the olive oil. Serve as a *mezze* dish, with warm *pita* bread.

SAMBUSAK
Cheese-filled pastry crescents

DOUGH
1/4 cup/80g butter, melted
1/4 cup/80g olive or vegetable oil
1/4 cup/80g water
1 teaspoon salt
2 cups/225g all-purpose/plain flour
1 egg yolk, or milk, to glaze
1 teaspoon sesame seeds

CHEESE FILLING
1 oz/225g white cheese (feta is ideal)
pepper
1 hard-boiled egg, diced

Mix the butter, oil, water and salt together in a bowl. Add the flour a tablespoon at a time, mixing thoroughly. Any lumps will gradually disappear. The consistency is right when pieces of dough flake away from the sides of the bowl and it can be shaped into a smooth ball. Pre-heat the oven to 375°F/190°C.

To make the filling, simply mix the cheese and other ingredients together.

To make the *sambusak*, break off walnut-size pieces of dough and roll them into circles about 3 inches/8cm across. Put a teaspoon of filling onto each circle, fold the dough over the filling, and crimp the edges together with finger and thumb. Take care not to overfill - the cheese mixture tends to expand during cooking.

Lay the *sambusak* side by side on an oiled baking sheet, brush with egg yolk or milk, and bake for 30 minutes or until golden brown. Makes about 20.

CARROT & SOUR CREAM COLD SOUP

3 tablespoons butter
1 onion, coarsely chopped
1 clove garlic
2 lbs/900g carrots, sliced
1/2 tablespoon each of ground turmeric, coriander, ginger and chili
2 cups/500ml vegetable stock
2 cups/500ml sour cream
1 cup/225g plain yogurt
scant 1/2 teaspoon salt
fresh chives, to garnish

Put the butter, onion, garlic, carrots and spices into a pressure cooker and simmer for 10 minutes. Add the stock, put the lid on and pressure cook for 15 minutes. Allow to cool, then liquidize and strain through a fine sieve. Add the sour cream, yogurt and salt, and chill well. Serve with a sprinkling of snipped chives.

◆ Sambusak *can make a hearty meal. Feta cheese gives* sambusak *a tangy taste and each bite is dipped in za'atar, a mixture of hyssop and spices.*

◆ *Freshly baked* sambusak *in one of many small, busy bakeries in Jaffa.*

FRIED GOAT'S CHEESE WITH MINT SALAD

12 oz/350g goat's cheese in a log, well chilled
flour
1 egg, lightly beaten and seasoned with thyme
and nutmeg
vegetable oil
garlic
1 small onion, finely chopped
1 tablespoon olive oil
1 tablespoon wine vinegar
dash tabasco
6 heaped tablespoons chopped fresh mint

Slice the cheese and dip the slices first in flour, then in beaten egg, then in flour again. Heat the oil in a skillet/frying pan until it just begins to smoke, then slide the cheese slices into the pan and cook on both sides until golden brown.

Rub the inside of a bowl with garlic, and mix together the chopped onion, olive oil, vinegar, tabasco and mint. Spoon the mixture onto individual plates and place the cheese slices on top. Makes 4 portions.

◆ Goats

grazing by

an olive tree

near Harduf,

in northern

Israel.

AVOCADO ORANGE CHEESECAKE
Unusual but delicious

7 oz/200g graham crackers/digestive biscuits
1/4 cup/50g melted butter
3 oranges
1 large avocado
juice of 1/2 lemon
3 oz/75g cream cheese
2 eggs, separated
2/3 cup/150ml sour cream
1/2 oz/15g gelatin
2 tablespoons sugar

Crush the crackers/biscuits, stir in the melted butter and press the mixture into the bottom of a 7-inch/18-cm cake pan. Grate the rind of one orange, squeeze the juice from two, and prepare a few peeled orange segments from the third. Remove several slices from the avocado and put them in water to a little lemon juice has been added - this prevents them blackening.

In a food precessor, blend together the rest of the avocado and lemon juice, the cream cheese, egg yolks, sour cream, orange rind and orange juice. Dissolve the gelatin in a little water and add it to the mixture, beating well. Whip/whisk the egg whites with the sugar until stiff, then fold them into the creamy orange/avocado mixture. Spoon the mixture into the cake pan, garnish with the orange segments and drained avocado slices, and refrigerate. Makes 12 generous servings.

◆ Fried goat's

cheese with

mint.

GREEK SALAD

As with watermelon and feta, this salad
has become a "native" of Israel.

1 romaine/cos or crisphead/iceberg lettuce
4 cucumbers
4 large, juicy tomatoes
1 onion, peeled
salt and pepper to taste
wine vinegar
olive oil
11 oz/300g feta cheese
1 teaspoon dried thyme
black olives, to garnish

Wash all the vegetables. Cut the lettuce
into 1-inch/2.5-cm cubes. Slice the onions
into rings. Cut all the other vegetables into
cubes or chunks the same size as the lettuce
(leave the cucumbers unpeeled). Divide
the lettuce among 4 big soup bowls, then
arrange the other vegetables on top. Season
with salt, pepper, vinegar and oil to taste.
Cut the cheese into cubes and put it on top.
Add the onion rings and a sprinkling of
dried thyme. Decorate each bowl with 4 or
5 black olives.

◆ *Feta cheese*

salad, an

Israeli version

of a Greek

recipe.

◆ *Waiting for a*

breeze. A slice of

sweet, juicy

watermelon is com-

plemented by feta

cheese and black

olives.

F I S H

No one ever forgets, even if he or she has enjoyed it only once, the aroma and flavor of freshly caught Mediterranean fish grilled over charcoal. The fish are not more exciting or flavorful than those caught in Boston

◆ *Yuki, a trout*

farmer, raises trout

in the choppy waters

of the Banias River.

The cold clear

waters originate in

the melted snow of

Mount Hermon.

or Le Havre or Hydra - in all honesty Israel's territorial waters offer a poor catch compared with other Mediterranean countries - but the direct and intense heat of the open fire, the nutty perfume of the smoke and the crispiness of the fish's skin seem to make all the difference. Charcoal-grilled fish can be sampled in any of thousands of restaurants from Alexandria to Athens, from Algiers to Istanbul, but the taste of Jaffa is unique. Here fish need only a hint of garlic, lemon juice and red pepper to be perfect.

◆ Fisherman's wharf in the port of Acre, one of Israel's biblical towns.

As you drive south along Tel Aviv's renovated Riviera, the ramparts of the old city of Jaffa rise from the tranquil sea. Jaffa is untouched by time. The city planners keep their distance. There is a quality of age and grace about the place that is better left untouched.

A few years ago a fisherman called Benny Raba came ashore and opened a fish restaurant. He is short and stocky and not at all the slim, trim fellow he was in his fishing days, but in the few years he has been in dry dock

he has become a walking status symbol. He drives a brand-new Mercedes with a car phone and wears gold bracelets and chains. He sits at his table facing the sea and holds court.

Benny's favourite pastime is recalling his seafaring days, when the sea was fierce and the fish were feisty. He cuts the air with chubby, leathery hands to illustrate his points, and as he sails down memory lane an attentive waiter covers the table with *mezze*, small colorful plates of appetizers such as *hummus*, *tahini*, *labaneh*, *tabbouleh*, eggplant purée, pickles, red hot peppers and other delights. Benny pushes a plate of fat, shiny olives towards his guests, urging them to try one, waiting anxiously for the verdict. The olives are meaty and tasty, and they blend well with the moist chunks of feta cheese.

Benny's religion is fresh fish. He will show you the eyes and say, "You can tell a fresh fish by its eyes." His fish are firm of body and bright of color, and do not flake and fall apart when they are deep-fried. No, Benny is not ashamed to deep-fry his fresh fish, although it seems that Israel is, in general, past its deep-frying days. Why fry a fish to a crisp if you can flirt with it? With a charcoal grill going full blast at every street corner, is it not a shame and a sin to fish & chip your fish?

◆ A fisherman mends a net torn by rocks off Jaffa harbor.

When he is in the mood or when the restaurant is quiet, Benny dons an apron and goes into his kitchen. Taking an ax to a huge gray mullet, he reduces it to bite-size pieces and grills them on skewers over an open fire. Before he serves them, he flambés them in arak, the local version of ouzo or Pernod.

Authentic, ethnic fish restaurants are a relatively new phenomenon in Israel. Until quite recently, Israelis were anything but adventurous when it came to fish. For generations, Jewish holidays called for fish, but it was fish ground and molded into gefilte fish - the smell was there, there was a even a soupçon of taste, but mainly it was just another patty covered with sauce. The Jews of Poland used to cover their fish with a jellied sauce made of sugar and almonds. And when it was not ground and sauced out of existence, fish was baked in the oven with vegetables and spices. When it finally arrived on the table, overcooked and falling off the bones, wives insisted that their husbands eat the heads. Since the most widely used fish in Jewish cooking was the impossible and dangerous carp, choking and coughing up bones was a customary part of all festival meals. Now we have discovered that carp is not the only fish worth eating, the excitement of the discovery is everywhere

◆ Back from an early morning excursion, Benny proudly displays a huge palamida. The large fish is cut into generous steaks.

evident. Diners are learning the names of local fish and pronouncing them with increasing confidence. They can tell a fresh fish from a tired one, a juicy one from an assemblage of skin and bones disguised as fish.

Trout are a new discovery. In northern Israel, in the Galilee region, there are numerous trout farms. The Dan and the Banias, which flow down from Mount Hermon into the Kinneret (Sea of Galilee), are two of the rivers whose cold choppy waters are used by trout farms. In spring, when the snow on Mount Hermon melts, the rivers are fierce. Now, in small pools and tanks strictly and scientifically supervised, Israeli trout grow to prize-winning proportions. They are sold locally or delivered weekly to the major cities.

Trout have caught on nicely. They are, in many ways, a fish for beginners - not too fishy, not too many bones, and easy to clean and cook. They are elegant, upmarket, easy to promote, and make a pleasant change from local gray mullet, red mullet and bream.

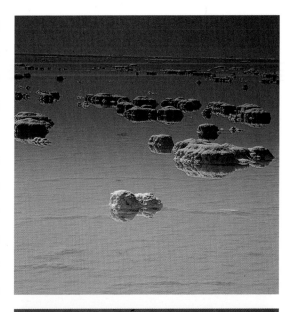

◆ *The Dead Sea.*

◆ *Eilat on the Red*
Sea is Israel's
southernmost
region. Since the
return of the
Sinai Desert to
Egypt, Eilat has
enjoyed an influx
of tourists.

It is a geographical wonder that a country as small as Israel possesses four potentially fishy realms: the Eastern Mediterranean, the Red Sea, the Kinneret, and the Dead Sea. But ecological abuse and neglect have made the last two barren; the Dead Sea is culinarily useless, except for salt, and the Kinneret holds little or no fish, not even the famous St. Peter's fish, now transplanted to fish farms. At one time most fishing in the Red Sea was done along the shores of Sinai, but since this stretch of sea was returned to Egypt it

◆ *Known for its
unique therapeu-
tic qualities, the
Dead Sea attracts
people from all
over the world.
A day covered in
mud does wonders
for the skin.*

◆ *Eli Avivi is self-
appointed head of
state of Achziv.
A stretch of white
sandy beach along
the Mediterranean,
Achziv is also the
site of a Club Med
village.*

◆ *Hammat Gader,*
  a kibbutz on the
  Golan, raises
  crocodiles pri-
  marily for export.
  A restaurant spe-
  cializing in croc
  meat is planned.

◆ *Deep-sea fishing*
  is forbidden in the
  Red Sea so divers
  use nets instead of
  air guns.

has been out of bounds to Israeli fisherman. So Israel's need for fish is now supplied by fish farms and deep fishing in the Mediterranean.

The Mediterranean contains an extraordinary variety of fish waiting to be tasted by those tired of the ubiquitous frozen mullet. Around the coast of Israel there is a passion - which becomes an obsession in the summer - for catching and eating all forms of seafood. Benny Raba gets very cross about "all the silly fuss in summer." In summer, he says, the sea is too warm. The fish are already parboiled when you take them out. To get good fish in summer a fisherman must sail deep and far and only a few fishermen do that. Why on earth, he asks bitterly, do Israelis associate fish with summer?

To befriend a fisherman or the owner of a fish restaurant means accepting some strange delicacies, all with that unmistakable sea taste of iodine. For stronger stomachs, there are fan mussels and sinewy squid. For the conservative, there are bright red mullet, needing no scaling or gutting, grilled with fragrant herbs. The grouper, which can grow to a great size in the safety of deep rock holes, has a delicate flavor, and the *palamida*, or lesser tuna, has a more subtle taste than its larger relative, as well as being one of the most beautiful fish in the Mediterranean.

The factor that unites all the countries of the Mediterranean is a similarity of recipes for cooking seafood. The Greeks claim that *bouillabaisse* was originally a hearty fisherman's soup or stew. And so it is, and alive and cooking in Jaffa. In Israel fish are also eaten baked, with or without vegetables, or fried whole or in slices, or charcoal-grilled, with many different sauces. They are also braised in the style known as *hreimeh*, or minced and made into loaves and patties cooked in tasty courts-bouillons. All of these cooking methods can be applied to most locally caught fish.

$\mathcal{F}$ I S H

◆ Mousht,

St. Peter's

fish, is

Israel's

leading

fish.

$\mathcal{R}ecipes$

RED MULLET WITH ORANGE BUTTER

*2 lbs/900g very fresh red mullet
rind and juice of 2 lbs/900g oranges
salt and pepper to taste
pinch of hot chili powder
1 clove garlic, minced
1 teaspoon sugar
2 tablespoons white wine
mixture of butter and oil for frying
1 cup/225g unsalted butter, melted*

If the red mullet are small, simply wash them. If they weigh more than 3 oz/75g, scale and clean them. Cut the orange rind into very thin strips, blanch it in boiling water for 2 minutes, then drain. Put the orange juice into a saucepan and add the salt, chili powder, garlic, sugar, wine and the blanched rind, and simmer until half the liquid has evaporated.

In the meantime, pat-dry the fish, sprinkle them with salt and pepper, and dip them in flour, shaking off any excess. Heat the butter/oil in a skillet/frying pan until it begins to smoke, then slide the fish into the pan. For a crispy result, do not try to fry too many fish at once. Fry for 5 minutes on each side, depending on size, then drain quickly on paper towels/kitchen paper. Transfer the fish to 4 pre-heated main course/8 pre-heated starter plates.

Remove the orange juice/spice mixture from the heat and stir in the melted butter, or simply transfer both to a glass jar, screw the top on, and shake vigorously to a smooth, semi-transparent consistency. Pour the sauce over the fish and serve.

BAKED GRAY MULLET

*3 or 4 cloves garlic
1 large green pepper, sliced very thin
4 tablespooons chopped fresh parsley
juice of 1 lemon
salt and freshly ground black pepper
3 tablespoons olive oil
1 onion, thinly sliced
1 gray mullet, about 3 lbs/1.4 kg, scaled and cleaned
lemon wedges, to garnish*

Chop most of the garlic very fine and mix it with the green pepper, parsley, lemon juice, salt, pepper and oil. Pour this mixture over the sliced onion, reserving a little to flavor the inside of the fish.

Cut one or two shallow slits in each side of the fish and insert the rest of the garlic, cut into slivers. Spoon the reserved onion-herb-garlic mixture inside the fish. Lay the fish in a baking dish, surrounded by the rest of the onion-herb-garlic marinade, and leave in a cool place for at least 30 minutes. Turn once so that both sides of the fish have a chance to absorb the marinade.

Pre-heat the oven to 375°F/190°C and bake the fish for about 30 minutes, basting it once or twice and turning it once. When the flesh flakes easily, it is cooked. Serve garnished with lemon wedges, with the cooked marinade as a sauce. Serves 4 or 5.

◆ *Red mullet with orange butter.*

TWO SAUCES FOR GRILLED FISH

Grilling is by far the most popular method of cooking fish in Israel.

LEMON-GARLIC SAUCE

3 tablespoons olive oil
2 tablespoons lemon juice
3 cloves garlic, minced
1/2 teaspoon salt
1/4 cup/60ml water

Heat the oil in a small saucepan. Add the lemon juice, garlic and salt, and simmer for 3 minutes. Allow to cool. Serve cold.

ONION-LEMON SAUCE FOR FISH

4 tablespoons olive oil
2 scallions/spring onions, shredded very fine
1/2 teaspoon salt
1 tablespoon vinegar
1 1/2 teaspoons harissa (see recipe p. 41)
1/2 cup/100ml water

Lightly sauté the onion in the oil. Add salt, vinegar and *harissa*, and mix well. Add the water and simmer for 3 minutes. Allow to cool. Serve cold.

WHOLE FISH ON THE SPIT

1/2 teaspoon paprika
4 tablespoons coriander seeds
6 cardamom pods
1 tablespoon anise or dill seeds
2 onions, chopped
2 cloves garlic, crushed
2 tablespoons chopped fresh mint
4 tablespoons chopped fresh parsley
1 green pepper, cored and thinly sliced
2/3 cup/150ml plain yogurt, whipped
juice of 1 lemon or lime
3 lbs/1.4kg fish (sea bass, gray mullet), cleaned, with heads and tails removed
salt and pepper
1/4 cup/60g clarified butter

Toast the paprika and coriander in a skillet/frying pan, then grind them up with the other spices. Add them to the onions, garlic, herbs and green pepper, and mix to a smooth paste with the yogurt and lemon juice.

Prick the fish all over and rub in the spice and herb mixture. Season with salt and pepper and allow to marinate for 1 hour.

Thread the fish onto a barbecue spit, with a pan underneath to catch the juices. Grill for 15 minutes or until the herb paste is dry. Baste with the pan juices, then raise the spit and cook for a further 25 minutes over a gentle heat, turning once.

The fish are cooked when they flake easily. Lower the spit to raise the intensity of the heat, baste the fish with the clarified butter and continue cooking until the skins are crisp. Serve at once, with salad and potatoes. Serves 6.

PALAMIDA
Marinated bonito/lesser tuna

Scale and clean the fish, slice them into 3/4-inch/2-cm pieces, and marinate overnight in the following mixture: 4 cups/1 liter water, 1/2 cup/100g salt, 1 teaspoon vinegar, 1 crushed clove garlic.

For an authentic Bulgarian Jewish breakfast, eat with onions, olives and thin slices of gray mullet roe, washed down with vodka.

◆ *Marinated palamida, stage two. The marinated fish is served with scallions, black olives and Turkish caviar (gray mullet roe sliced very thin).*

◆ *Victor's is a delicatessen store deep in the heart of the Levinsky market in Tel Aviv. It is a typical deli specializing in smoked fish and herrings.*

◆ *Marinated palamida, stage one. The fish is cut into chunks and covered with sea salt.*

TROUT BARBECUED IN GRAPE LEAVES

8 trout, 8-10 oz/225-275g each
1 cup/225ml olive oil
1/4 cup/60ml fresh lemon juice
scant tablespoon minced capers
2 tablespoons minced fresh parsley
1 tablespoon fresh chives, snipped small
1 teaspoon minced fresh basil
1/2 teaspoon minced fresh rosemary
8 sprigs fresh thyme
40 large grape/vine leaves, fresh or preserved
1 lemon, cut into wedges, to garnish
sprigs of fresh herbs, to garnish

Top, tail and bone the trout, leaving them otherwise whole. Then score them on both sides at 2 1/2 inch/6cm intervals, holding the knife at an angle of 30° and cutting a quarter of the way through the flesh.

Mix together the olive oil, lemon juice, capers and herbs and rub this mixture generously over the fish, inside and out. Put a sprig of thyme in each fish, then wrap each one in 5 grape leaves, overlapping them so that they entirely envelop the fish. Secure with string at 1-inch/2.5-cm intervals.

Prepare the barbecue. When the coals are ready, scatter soaked *mesquite* or fruitwood chips on top. When they begin to smolder, place the fish on the grill/rack and cover with foil. If the fish are about 1 inch/2.5-cm thick, they will take about 10 minutes to cook; if thicker, proportionately longer. Turn once during cooking.

To serve, remove the string but leave the grape leaves on, and garnish with lemon wedges and fresh herbs. Serves 8.

TROUT WITH POMEGRANATE

1 large pomegranate
4 fresh trout
salt and pepper to taste
pinch cardamom
1 onion, chopped
1/2 cup/100g butter
2 cloves garlic, minced
1 cup/100g pecans, coarsely chopped
2 tablespoons vinegar

Cut the pomegranate in half and tap rather than scoop out the seeds so that they remain intact. Wash and clean the fish. With trout, it is possible to break the backbone near the head and pull it out whole, leaving the fish intact but deboned.

Lightly fry the onions in a little of the butter. Season the inside of the fish with salt, pepper and cardamom to taste, then stuff them with the pomegranate seeds, fried onion, garlic and chopped pecans, and put a knob of butter in each. If necessary, close the openings with toothpicks/cocktail sticks.

Butter an ovenproof dish and lay the fish in it. Bake in an oven pre-heated to 400°F/ 200°C for 12 minutes. Serve on a bed of mustard and cress or watercress, garnished with the rest of the pomegranate seeds.

◆ *Trout with pomegranate on a bed of cress.*

GEFILTE FISH
Traditional poached fishballs

2 lbs/900g fresh carp
1 slice stale challah or 1/2 cup/60g matzo flour
1 hard-boiled egg
2 tablespoons oil
1 large onion
2 eggs
salt, black pepper and sugar to taste

BROTH/STOCK
4 carrots, sliced
2 onions, sliced
4 cups/1 liter water
salt, pepper and sugar to taste

Wash the fish and cut it into slices, reserving the roe for future use. Sprinkle the slices with salt and refrigerate for 1 hour. Soak the *challah* in water, and then drain.

Using a sharp knife, skin the fish, saving any unbroken rings of skin. Discard only the main bones. Ignoring all the other bones, grind/mince the fish twice with the hard-boiled egg and *challah* to achieve a smooth consistency. At this stage some cooks would add 8 oz/225g of pike fillet, a few almonds or a raw carrot, but these are optional.

Now blend in the 2 eggs, oil, salt and pepper, and sugar to taste - knowing the powerful emotions aroused by the subject of how much sugar gefilte fish should contain, we do not dare specify the amount of sugar to be added here - and refrigerate.

Put all the broth ingredients into a large saucepan, bring to a boil and cook for 30 minutes. Add the fish's head and continue to simmer. Meanwhile, form the chilled fish mixture into balls, wetting your hands to prevent the mixture sticking to them. If you managed to save any rings of skin, stuff them with the mixture too. Smooth them with your wet hands and slide them one by one, with the other balls, into the simmering broth. Cover the saucepan, leaving a small gap between the lid and the saucepan, and simmer for 2 hours. When cool, put in the refrigerator.

To serve, put 2 or 3 balls on each plate with a slice of carrot on top and some of the jellied broth. Serve the fish head to the head of the family. *Challah* and horseradish relish (see recipes p. 90 and 41) are an absolute must with gefilte fish. Makes enough for 8 starter portions.

HERRINGS IN SOUR CREAM

1 cup/225ml heavy/double cream
2 tablespoons sugar
2 tablespoons white wine vinegar
10 fat herrings
1 medium red onion, sliced very thin

Fillet the herrings and remove the skin, then cut each fillet into 5 or 6 pieces. Whip/whisk the sugar into the cream and stir in the vinegar. Put the fish into a glass jar, with layers of onion in between, and pour in the cream. Cover and refrigerate. Use within 10 days. Makes 20 servings.

◆ *Sunset over the Kinneret, Israel's only freshwater lake.*

POACHED SEA BASS MARINATED IN LEMON & BASIL

rind of 1 lemon, pared off in strips
6 fillets sea bass, about 8 oz/225g each
1/2 cup/100ml fresh lemon juice
1/3 cup/80ml white wine vinegar
1 1/2 teaspoons salt
1/2 teaspoon sugar
1 1/2 cups/350ml extra-virgin olive oil
3 tablespoons finely choppped basil, plus sprigs
of basil to garnish
2 large cloves garlic, chopped
2 teaspoons dried hot red pepper flakes
1 cup/225ml dry white wine
2 bay leaves
2 sprigs parsley
4 cups/1 liter water
red bell pepper, finely chopped, to garnish

Put the lemon rind in the bottom of a shallow dish large enough hold all the bass fillets flat. Skin the fillets and cut them crosswise into strips about 1 1/4 inches/3cm wide.

Whip/whisk together the lemon juice, vinegar, 1/2 teaspoon salt, sugar and oil until the mixture emulsifies (thickens and goes cloudy), then whip in half the chopped basil, the garlic and the red pepper flakes.

In a large saucepan, combine the wine, bay leaves, parsley and the rest of the salt with the water, and bring to a boil. Turn down the heat so that the liquid is just simmering, then slide half a dozen strips of bass into the liquid and poach them for 1– 1 1/2 minutes or until the flesh is just firm. Remove with a slotted spoon and transfer to the dish with the lemon rind. Poach the rest of the fish in the same way.

Pour the marinade over the fish, cover, and allow to marinate overnight in the refrigerator.

Let the fish stand at room temperature for 1 hour before serving. Transfer the fish slices to individual plates, strain the marinade through a fine sieve, whip it well to emulsify it, and drizzle it over the fish. Sprinkle with the red bell pepper and the rest of the basil, and garnish with basil sprigs. Serves 8 to 10.

MOUSHT WITH TAHINI
St. Peter's fish with sesame sauce

St. Peter's fish (*mousht* in Arabic) is a Sea of Galilee fish. It is a bony, tasty fish not unlike sea bream.

2 onions, sliced
1/4 cup/60ml vegetable oil
4 small mousht (or trout), cleaned
1/2 cup/100ml tahini/sesame seed paste
2 tablespoons lemon juice
1 clove garlic, crushed
salt and pepper
blanched vegetables
and sesame seeds, to garnish

Pre-heat the oven to 325°F/170°C. Using a large skillet/frying pan, sauté the onion in the oil until it is soft, then add the fish and cook them for 1 minute on each side so that they absorb some of the onion flavor.

Blend together the *tahini*, lemon juice and garlic. Transfer the fish and the onions to an ovenproof dish, sprinkle them with salt and pepper, and coat them with the *tahini* mixture. Bake, uncovered, for 30 minutes or until the fish flake easily. Garnish with blanched vegetables and sesame seeds.
Serves 4.

◆ Mousht

with tahini:

St. Peter's fish

with sesame

sauce.

BREAD

◆ *Large, flat Iraqi* pita *are baked in the traditional* taboon, *a clay oven, in Ashtanur bakery, Jerusalem. The dough is flattened against the interior of the* taboon *and falls off when ready.*

I f *falafel* were not such an in-tegral part of Israeli folklore, bread - any bread - would be the king of Israeli food. But dethroning *falafel* would be a political move requiring great bold-ness and courage. Opposition would be

vocal and nasty. Yet we eat more bread than *falafel*, and how would *falafel* survive without *pita* bread? What other vehicle is there for those tasty little patties and handfuls of salad?

I am biased when it comes to bread. Bread is in my blood. I am a baker's son, and would have been a third-generation baker if I had not betrayed my heritage. My father sold the family's 50-year-old bakery when he became certain that I was a lost cause. He was as much to blame as I was, because this is what he told me about bread. People eat it all the time. It's so ordinary that they stop noticing it. It's invisible. When you bake an invisible staple, you too become invisible. People only notice you when your oven breaks down and your bread is ruined. Then they hate you. People who have never appreciated you resent you the first chance they get. Also, it's a hard, backbreaking job being a baker. Creativity does not come into it. Bread is not about creativity. It is about flour and water and yeast and the way they rise in the steam room and then brown in the oven.

We have always eaten bread in this country. When Jerusalem was under siege in the '48 war, everything stopped. No one came or went. The only convoys that got through were trucks bearing water and bread. When they didn't get through, people baked their own bread, if they had the flour and the yeast. Bread is what you eat when you have no other food.

Even in these affluent times, few Israelis dine without bread. Bread even enjoys a government subsidy - that is how important it is. Israelis have never

◆ *In Israel, the term "black bread" refers to the most common bread. This is subsidized by the goverment, so anyone can afford it.*

paid the full price of a loaf of bread. By subsidizing bread, the government shows a proper regard for one of the last tenets of socialism. Whatever happens, the government implies, we will always have bread. We will never starve.

If bread is the uncrowned king of Israel, then *challah* is the queen. *Challah* is the traditional Jewish egg-rich braided bread which is ritually blessed and served every Friday night when the members of observant families get together to re-establish the kinship and continuity of family life. On Friday nights one does not talk shop. Business matters are forbidden as a subject of conversation. The name *challah* actually means "the priest's share" and derives from the fact that a little piece of dough is symbolically removed from the main body of dough before it is shaped into loaves and put in the oven. The "priests's share" must rise on its own and be baked separately from the rest, and when it is baked it must be charred or burned beyond redemption - it is a sacrifice and not meant to be eaten. *Challah* is the bread we eat on festive occasions such as holidays and weddings. A special blessing involving a *challah*, usually quite a large one baked specially for the occasion, is part of Jewish weddings. Bread and salt are traditional gifts at a Jewish house-warming.

The heir-apparent is the *pita*, such an essential part of Israeli eating that it is hard to imagine life without it. Most starters or *mezze* dishes rely heavily on *pita*. Why use a fork to eat your *hummus* or *tahini* when you can use a hand-torn, edible scoop? *Hummus*-scooping is an art honed over many years. We expect *pita* to be there. We reach for it without even looking up from our newspapers.

◆ *Simcha Haddad of Netanya still uses the taboon to bake bread in her back yard.*

◆ *General view of the flat, fertile Jezreel Valley.*

A cultural war is now in progress between the followers of *pita* and the followers of bread. The two staples represent two cultures, Ashkenazi and Sephardic, in the process of become one nation. Jews who came to Israel from Arab countries, Sephardim, have always eaten *pita*. Ashkenazim, from Russia, Poland and Germany, are addicted to bread and have tried hard to preserve their heritage, but their efforts at baking the traditional breads of the old countries have seldom been successful. Over the years they have given up. Bread needs so much attention, with all the rising and kneading and rising again. Now they have to make do with local bread.

In other words, the bread versus *pita* war is not going bread's way at the moment, although the Tunisian open sandwich - a whole loaf of bread

cut in two, hollowed out and filled with salad, tuna, salami, and saturated with virgin olive oil - seems to be standing its ground, principally for heroic reasons. Gone are the days when traditional bakers scoffed at the quickly-made, non-rising Arab *pita*. Now there are specialized *pita* bakeries that do booming business day and night - long lines form in front of them in the dark hours - and the *pitas* they produce are not plain or ordinary. Adapting the principle of the pizza, Israeli *pita* makers have started to add different

◆ *An old*

flour mill

in the

village of

Shefar'am.

toppings. *Pita* with the salty herb mixture known as *za'atar* is a big hit. Then there are *pita*-pizza topped with egg, mushrooms, basil and tomato, and a dozen other flavors....This is the age of the *pita* and most Israelis eat *pita* in great quantities, whatever their country of origin.

B R E A D

◆ *The popular Abulafia bakery in Jaffa specializes in doughy* pitas *with assorted toppings. Abulafia also bakes bagels.*

Recipes

CHALLAH
Sweet braided bread eaten on the Sabbath

1 1/2 tablespoons dried yeast
1/2 cup/100ml lukewarm water, to activate yeast
1 teaspoon sugar
3 eggs
1/2 cup/100g sugar
1 1/2 cups/350ml lukewarm warm water, to mix with dough
1/2 cup/125ml vegetable oil
1 1/2 teaspoons salt
9 cups/1kg all-purpose/plain flour
2 eggs, beaten with 2 tablespoons water
sesame or poppy seeds, to garnish

Combine the yeast, the 1/2 cup/125ml lukewarm water and the sugar, and set aside. In a large mixing bowl, beat together the eggs and sugar, then add the 1 1/2 cups of lukewarm water, oil and salt. Stir in the frothing yeast mixture and beat well. Using a wooden spoon, beat in half the flour, adding a heaped tablespoonful at a time and beating well after each addition. At this stage, the dough will be sticky. Add half the remaining flour, beating in a tablespooonful at a time as before. The dough should now leave the sides of the bowl.

Dredge the rest of the flour onto a work surface, remove the dough from the bowl and knead it for 10 minutes until all the flour has been absorbed. Return the dough to the bowl, cover it with a damp towel, and let it rise in an unheated oven with the door closed for 1 hour or until it has more or less doubled in size.

Punch down the dough and divide it into three equal portions. Cut each portion into three and shape the thirds into long sausages. Braid/plait the sausages together to make three loaves.

Place the loaves on a greased and floured baking sheet, cover, and leave them to rise for about 1 1/2-2 hours, or until they have nearly doubled in volume. Pre-heat the oven to 400°F/210°C.

Brush each loaf with the egg and water mixture, sprinkle with poppy or sesame seeds, and bake for 15 minutes until golden. Tap the loaves on the bottom to see if they sound hollow - if they don't, give them another few minutes. When they do sound hollow, leave them in the oven for another 5 minutes. Cool on a wire rack. Makes 3 loaves.

◆ Challah *comes in many shapes and forms. Round* challah *with poppy seeds is hard to slice with a knife. Kids love to tear them to pieces.*

◆ *A slice of sweet* challah *with raisins.*

90

PITA
Middle Eastern flat bread/pocket bread

1 tablespoon dried yeast
1 tablespoon salt
2 tablespoons honey
2 1/3-3 cups/600-700ml lukewarm water
6-7 cups/700-800g all-purpose/plain flour

Mix together the yeast, honey and 1/2 cup/ 125ml lukewarm water in a small bowl and allow to stand for 10 minutes in a warm place. Put 4 cups/450g of the flour into a large mixing bowl, add the frothing yeast mixture and 2 cups/500ml lukewarm water, and beat vigorously for a minute or two. Now add the salt and half the remaining flour and beat again.

On a lightly floured board, knead the dough for 10 minutes, adding more flour if necessary to make a medium stiff dough. Place the dough in a lightly greased bowl, cover, and leave in a warm, draft-free place to double in volume - this should take about 1 hour. Pre-heat the oven to 450°F/230°C.

Punch down the dough, knead it again, then divide it into 12 equal portions, rolling each one into a ball with your hands. Roll the balls of dough into flat circles about 5 inches/13cm across and 1/4 inch/0.6cm thick, place the circles on an ungreased baking sheet, cover and allow to rise for 10 minutes. Cook on the bottom rack of the oven for 8 minutes, or until the bottoms are pale brown. If no pocket appears, raise the oven temperature; if too brown, spray with water. Allow to cool, then put into plastic bags and refrigerate or freeze.

Pita bread should be served warm. Three minutes in a pre-heated 350°F/180°C oven should be enough to warm them through. Any longer, and they become rock hard! Makes 12.

◆ *Abulafia's*

best, a tray of

pita, bagels,

ka'ahks

(bagels with

sesame

seeds), pita

with egg,

za'atar,

onion and

olives, and

Iraqi pita.

SESAME PITA TOASTS

*2 rounds pita bread about
6 inches/15cm across
3 oz/80g sesame seeds, lightly toasted
3 tablespoons unsalted butter, softened
salt*

Pre-heat the oven to 375°/190°F. Cut each *pita* into quarters, then separate the quarters so that you have 8 more or less triangular pieces of bread. Dredge the sesame seeds onto a flat surface, spread the rough sides of the *pita* triangles with butter and press them, butter side down, onto the sesame seeds.

Arrange the triangles, sesame side up, on a baking sheet and bake in the oven for 8 - 10 minutes or until the toasts are crisp. Transfer the toasts to a cooling rack, sprinkle them with salt to taste, and serve warm or at room temperature.

CHILDREN'S PIZZA

*1 pita
1/2 cup/100ml tomato sauce
1/2 cup/80g pitted olives
1 bell pepper, sliced
5 oz/150g canned tuna or sweetcorn, optional
7 oz/200g Gruyère cheese*

Made by children, this can be a creative experience. First separate the *pita* into perfect round halves. Spread each half with tomato sauce, arrange the olives, pepper and canned tuna or sweetcorn on top, and cover with cheese, grated or thinly sliced. Put under the broiler/grill until the cheese is nicely melted. Chill and serve.

PITA WITH ONION & POPPY SEEDS

*2 oz/60g fresh yeast
1 teaspoon sugar
salt
1/2 cup/100ml lukewarm water
8 1/4 cups/950g all-purpose/plain flour
3 tablespoons oil
3 eggs, lightly beaten
3 onions, finely chopped
1/2 cup/100g poppy seeds*

Dissolve the yeast, sugar and a pinch of salt in the lukewarm water. Cover and leave in a warm place for 10 minutes until the mixture becomes frothy.

Put the flour into a large mixing bowl, make a well in the middle and pour in the yeast mixture, oil and 2 of the beaten eggs. Knead well. Cover with a towel, and put in a warm place for 30 minutes to allow the dough to rise.

Rub a little oil on your hands and roll the dough into about two dozen walnut-sized balls. Place the balls on a floured surface and roll them out into circles about 2 1/2 inches/7 cm across. Sprinkle each circle with onion, poppy seeds and a little salt, lightly pressing them into the dough with the rolling pin. Brush with the rest of the beaten egg. Cover and allow to rise for 30 minutes. Bake in a hot oven - 400°F/210°C - until golden brown.

Makes about 24.

BAGEL/KA'AHK
Pastry rings with cumin and coriander

4 cups/450g all-purpose/plain flour
1 teaspoon salt
1/2 oz/15g fresh yeast, or half this amount of
dried yeast
1 1/4 cups/300ml lukewarm water
pinch sugar
4 oz/100g unsalted butter or margarine, melted
1/2 teaspoon ground cumin
1/2 teaspoon ground coriander
1 egg, lightly beaten
sesame seeds

Dissolve the yeast in 2 tablespoons lukewarm water, add the sugar, and leave for 10-15 minutes.

Sift the salt, cumin and coriander into the flour, make a well in the middle and pour in the melted butter and frothing yeast mixture. Knead to a dough, adding the water a tablespoon at a time. Knead for 10 -15 minutes until the dough is smooth and comes away from the sides of the bowl. Cover the bowl with a damp cloth and leave in a warm place for 2 hours or until the dough has doubled in volume. Pre-heat the oven to 350°F/180°C.

Working on a floured surface, roll walnut-sized pieces of dough into thin 4 x 6 inch/10 x 15cm rectangles. Roll each rectangle into a cigar shape and bring the ends together to form a circle - press the ends firmly together with a little water. Arrange on a greased baking sheet, leaving 1 inch/ 2.5cm or so between each *ka'ahk*. Brush with the beaten egg and sprinkle with sesame seeds. Bake for 25-30 minutes until crisp and golden brown. Makes 20.

PRETZELS

1 oz/30 g active dry yeast
1 tablespoon sugar
1 cup/225ml lukewarm water
3 cups/350g sifted all-purpose/plain flour
2 tablespoons butter, softened
1/2 teaspoon salt
4 teaspoons baking soda
4 cups/1 liter water
coarse salt or sesame seeds, to garnish

Dissolve the yeast and a little of the sugar in the lukewarm water. When the mixture is frothing nicely, add it to the flour, butter and salt, and knead, knead, knead. Cover the dough with a cloth and allow it to rise to nearly double the volume. Punch it down, divide it into 12 equal portions and roll each one out into a ribbon 1/2 inch/1cm thick. Loop each ribbon into a figure of eight and leave in a warm place, covered with a cloth, to rise again. Pre-heat the oven to 450°F/ 230°C.

Dissolve the baking soda in the 4 cups/1 liter water and bring to a boil. Slide each pretzel into the boiling water and boil until it floats - about 1 minute. Remove with a fish slice and place on a baking sheet for 12 minutes. Before baking, sprinkle with coarse salt or sesame seeds. Bake until golden brown.

Although pretzels are delicious fresh, they will keep for up to 1 week. They are best eaten with butter.

◆ *A "hero" sandwich, a favorite of Israeli construction workers. It has everything in it, on a 700g loaf of black bread.*

MLAWAH
Flaky bread

3 cups/350g all-purpose/plain flour
1/4 teaspoon baking powder
1cup/225ml water
1cup/225ml butter, melted and clarified
1/2 teaspoon salt
1 teaspoon sugar
1 teaspoon vinegar, optional

Sift the baking powder into the flour, make a well in the center and add water, 1 tablespoon of the butter, salt, sugar and vinegar (if desired). Knead to a smooth elastic consistency. Cut into 6 equal portions, and allow to "rest" in a cool place for 20 minutes. Flatten each piece to a round the size of a *pita* - patience is a virtue here since the dough is springy and resists stretching and flattening! Liberally brush each round with the melted butter, then roll it into a tight sausage shape. Allow the rolls to rest for 20 minutes. Repeat the flattening, rolling and brushing procedure twice more, waiting 20 minutes between rolling and re-flattening. The final results should be flat and round like *pita*.

Using a non-stick skillet/frying pan, fry the *mlawah* on both sides until golden brown, flipping them over at half time. Serve with freshly puréed tomatoes and *zhoug*.

Mlawah freeze well. Just put waxed/greaseproof paper between them and seal them in a freezer bag.

LAHUHUA
Yemenite sponge bread

1 oz/25g yeast
3 cups/700ml lukewarm water
1 tablespoon sugar
3 1/2 cups/450g all-purpose/plain flour, sifted
1/2 teaspoon salt
5 tablespoons melted butter or shortening/lard

Dissolve the yeast in a little of the water. When it is frothing, combine it with the rest of the ingredients. Mix well, cover with a cloth and leave to rise in a warm place for 1 hour. Mix again, re-cover and leave for another hour.

Use a small non-stick skillet/frying pan to cook *lahuhua*. Start each pancake in a cold skillet, then cook for 2 minutes over a medium heat, then move the skillet to a very low heat and continue cooking for another 4 minutes. Cook on one side only.

Lahuhua are traditionally served with soups and stews. They are spongy and savoury, and not difficult to make.

◆ *Wheat*

harvest in

the Jezreel

Valley.

◆ *Fresh* pita

being baked

in the ancient

village of

Pequi'in.

The thin

rounds of

dough are

placed on hot

metal, flipped

over and

quickly

removed.

MEDITERRANEAN OLIVE ROLLS

1/2 oz/15g dried yeast
1 teaspoon sugar
1/2-1 teaspoon freshly ground black pepper
1 cup/225ml lukewarm water
3/4 cup/80g buckwheat flour
3 cups/350g all-purpose/plain flour
12 oz/350g brine-cured black olives, pitted and
coarsely chopped
2 tablespoons extra-virgin olive oil

Mix the yeast, sugar and pepper with the water and allow to stand for 10 minutes.

Put the buckwheat flour and the all-purpose flour into a mixing bowl, make a well in the middle and add the frothing yeast mixture, the oil and the chopped olives. Mix to a soft, sticky dough. Transfer the dough to a floured surface and knead gently for 2 minutes. Dust with flour, return to the mixing bowl, cover with plastic wrap/cling film and leave in a warm place for at least 45 minutes or until the dough has nearly doubled in size.

Turn the dough out onto a floured surface, cut it into quarters, roll each quarter into a ball, and cut each ball into four - you should now have 16 pieces of dough of equal size. With floured hands, shape the pieces into balls and arrange on an oiled baking sheet. Put in a warm place for 30-40 minutes to nearly double in volume. Preheat the oven to 400°F/210°C.

Before you put the rolls in the oven, make a shallow slash in the top of each. Bake in the lower third of the oven for 20-25 minutes or until the bottoms sound hollow when you tap them. Cool on a rack.
Makes 16.

FATTOUSH
Vegetable and herb salad with toasted pieces of bread

1 large cucumber, chopped
5 tomatoes, chopped
10 scallions/spring onions, chopped
1 small green pepper, chopped
1 tablespoon chopped parsley
1 tablespoon chopped coriander leaves, optional
1/2 tablespoons chopped fresh mint
1 clove garlic, crushed
6 tablespoons olive oil
juice of 2 lemons
1/2 teaspoon salt
1/4 teaspoon black pepper
2 pita, toasted and broken
into small pieces

Prepare all the vegetables and make sure the herbs are chopped very fine. Put them into a large salad bowl, add the oil, lemon juice, salt and pepper, and toss well. Chill until ready to serve, and at the last minute stir in the toasted pieces of bread.

Serves 5 or 6.

◆ Fattoush,

vegetable

and herb

salad with

pieces of

toasted

pita.

RADITIONAL DISHES

Go east young man and bring back a warm, fragrant pot of cholent. Weekends are made for take-aways and if you bring your own pot, there are many restaurants that will fill it for you.

Israel's two most dominant culinary traditions, European and Sephardic/Arab, meet and blend in the casserole. The Jewish observance of the Sabbath, when cooking is forbidden, and the Arab penchant for

◆ *A view of*

Mea She'arim,

Jerusalem's

orthodox

Jewish

quarter.

slow cooking have led to a comfortable convergence. Casseroles are one of the pillars of Israeli cuisine. By casseroles I mean dishes which require a whole night of cooking in a very low oven, dishes of lamb and chicken which are the staples of North African cuisine, and Arab meat dishes brought to table in large bowls.

From nightfall on Friday, Jews are not allowed to use electricity or to light a fire, which means that all the Sabbath food has to be prepared in advance or put in a warm oven overnight. Food is the main attraction of the Sabbath. Israelis never work on Saturdays and, since orthodox Jews are forbidden to drive, most of the day is spent at home. Special Sabbath dishes have been devised over the centuries, dishes that do not compromise taste and appeal for the sake of observance, but by the very nature of the slow cooking process most of them are heavy and substantial.

Meat and potatoes in a special stew called *cholent* are the trademark of Eastern European Jews. Spicy chicken and lamb *tagines* are typical of Moroccan Jews. *Jihnoon* and *kubbaneh*, which are dough-based, are part of Yemenite Jewish cuisine. All of them go into the oven on Friday night, to be consumed during the Sabbath. The Yemenites start earlier than others; *kubbaneh*, a spongy, spicy bread, is eaten for breakfast, to be joined later by *jihnoon*.

As a rule of thumb, slow-cooked food is usually eaten slowly. There is nothing fresh or crisp or sparkling about it, and there is no point in eating it quickly. Strong Turkish coffee and tea with mint are served with it.

◆ *Entrance*

Arab and Jewish traditional cooking are alike in their refusal to allow any change in the role of women as cooks and servants. The Israeli who returns from temple expecting his food to be on the table has much in

to a public

bath house

in Mea

She'arim.

common with the Arab who never enters the kitchen and never offers to help. While orthodox Jews demand their food and do nothing except pray over it and eat it, Arab men are in charge once the food actually reaches the table. An Arab woman never leaves the kitchen during a meal, whether her husband is dining alone or with guests. Women and children invariably eat in the kitchen. Out front, in the dining room, the Arab man hovers around his guests. He fills their glasses. He fills their plates. He refills their plates at the slightest sign of a dent in the small mountains of rice and meat he has set before them. He urges them to eat whenever their attention wanders....

◆ *Bible class in Mea She'arim.*

Most of the recipes given in this chapter are made in pots of one kind or another. All of them are braised or stewed or baked very slowly, usually covered. They are, by their nature, food for winter. *Cholent* is a typical Eastern European dish, but it also has North African and Iraqi variants. The slow-cooking casserole has evolved wherever Jews have lived. The Morrocans eat *dfeena* and the Iraqis have *tabyeet* - both are versions of *cholent*.

Cholent and its relatives are served in large pots cosily placed in the center of the table so that the whole family can help themselves and come back for more. They are the focus of social occasions. A clear soup, vegetables, condiments and pickles are usually served with them.

A place of honor is reserved for *couscous*, the national dish of Morocco. *Couscous* is also popular in Algeria and Tunisia, and in Paris, where *couscous* joints have long provided bargain meals for students and tourists. *Couscous* and its accompanying condiments and salads were brought to Israel by North African Jews in the 1950s, and the genre continues to flourish.

◆ *A heder or classroom for little boys in Mea She'arim.*

The word *couscous*, as used above, describes a combination of steamed grain, stewed meat (usually lamb), poultry or fish, and vegetables, or sometimes only steamed grain and vegetables. The grain itself is also called

couscous, and the hourglass-shaped vessel in which the dish is traditionally cooked is called a *couscousier*. When the *couscous* grain is taken from the steamer part of the *couscousier*, fluffed up, heaped on a platter and decorated with fragrant stew, the result is wonderfully satisfying, addictive even. Craig Claiborne has called *couscous* "one of the dozen greatest dishes in the world."

◆ *A couscousier, the authentic vessel in which to cook* couscous.

Couscous is usually served in a flat bowl or deep plate so that you can pour the stew broth over it. Flat *pita* bread is torn into pieces and used to scoop up the grain and stew, and then to mop up the juices in the bottom of the bowl. The condiment most frequently eaten with *couscous* is a paste based on red chili peppers called *harissa*. Moroccan cooks will diligently wash, drain and rake *couscous* with their bare hands for 20 to 30 minutes to add moisture and also get rid of any lumps. Then they steam it in a *couscousier*, toss it in cold salted water, and steam it again. There is a purpose to all this: the grains become remarkably fluffy and absorb the flavors from the vapors that rise from the stew bubbling beneath. But *couscous* does not have to be a career. You can buy quick cooking *couscous* from most specialty food stores and delicatessens.

Although most of the recipes in this chapter are not uniquely Israeli, they symbolize the way in which Jews from different cultures have assimilated here. It seems that food is the great glue that keeps us together.

$\mathcal{T}$ R A D I T I O N A L

D I S H E S

◆ *A crock of*

gold.

Cholent

is a meal in

itself.

Recipes

COUSCOUS WITH LAMB

3 lbs/1.5kg lamb, cut into chunks
1 tablespoon salt
1 teaspoon freshly ground black pepper
4 whole cloves, or 1/4 teaspoon ground cloves
1 teaspoon turmeric
2 bay leaves
4 large carrots (2 diced and 2 sliced)
4 onions (2 diced and 2 sliced)
2 sticks celery, chopped
12 pints/5.5 liters water
1 small cabbage, sliced
2 zucchini/courgettes, cut into bite-size pieces
2 turnips, cubed
10 oz/275g pumpkin, cut into large cubes
1/2 cup/75g raisins
2 lbs/900g quick-cooking couscous
1 lb/450g cooked chickpeas, drained

Put the lamb, salt, pepper, cloves, turmeric, bay leaves, diced carrots, diced onions and chopped celery into a *couscousier* or pan wide and deep enough to support a steamer or colander, and cover with water. Bring to a boil, lower the heat, and simmer for nearly 1 hour, or until the lamb is tender.

Pour the broth/stock through a strainer and reserve. Remove the meat from the strainer and reserve. Discard the vegetables.

Clean the *couscousier* or pan and return the reserved broth to it. Now add the sliced carrots, sliced onions, cabbage, zucchini, turnips, pumpkin and raisins. Partially cover the pan, and simmer for 5 minutes, or until the vegetables are tender. Meanwhile cook the *couscous* according to the directions on the packet. Add the reserved lamb and the drained chickpeas to the broth, then place the *couscous* container over the broth and turn up the heat so that the steam from the broth rises through the *couscous*. Steam for 20 minutes or according to directions, then heap the *couscous* onto a serving platter or onto individual plates and arrange the meat and vegetables on top. Spoon over a small amount of broth, and serve the rest in a jug. Serve with moroccan carrot salad (see recipe p. 34).

Serves 10 to 12.

◆ *Moroccan carrot salad is a traditional complement to couscous. See recipe page 34.*

◆ *Moroccan couscous with lamb. The golden semolina grains can be topped with all manner of broths and stews - lamb, chicken, fish and vegetables.*

ASHKENAZI CHOLENT

A layered hotpot of beans, chicken, marrow bones, dumpling and potatoes

12 medium potatoes
2 tablespoons salt
8oz/ 225g dry lima/butter beans
8oz/ 225g red kidney or adzuki beans
4 large onions, sliced
2 tablespoons vegetable oil
5 beef marrow bones
2 lbs/900g beef shoulder, cut into large cubes
1 cup/225g barley, washed
2 tablespoons sugar
2 tablespoons water
salt and pepper

CHOLENT KUGEL

1 onion, sliced
mixture of vegetable oil, margarine
& chicken fat
flour
slice of challah *bread (see recipe p. 90), soaked*
in water then squeezed dry
chicken soup powder
salt and pepper
1 egg, beaten
water

Peel the potatoes and soak them in water, with the 2 tablespoons salt, for 2 hours. Soak the beans in unsalted water for 2 hours, then drain them and season with salt and pepper. Season the marrow bones and beef with salt and pepper.

To make the kugel, sauté the onion in the oil/margarine/chicken fat, stir into the flour, add the *challah*, soup powder, salt and pepper, and knead to an elastic dough with the egg and water, adding more water if necessary. Roll the dough into a log shape, put it into a roasting bag, and prick a few holes in the bag.

In a large deep pan, sauté the 4 large onions in the oil. Remove from the heat and add, layered in the following order, the beans, the marrow bones and beef, the barley, the kugel in its roasting bag, and the potatoes.

Melt the sugar in a little water, turn up the heat and cook until the sugar turns dark brown. Stir in 2 tablespoons water, and immediately pour over the *cholent*. Add just enough water to cover all the ingredients, bring to a boil, and simmer briskly for 30 minutes. Cover the pan and transfer to a very low oven to cook overnight.

The *cholent* kugel is usually served separately from the *cholent*, cut into slices like a cake. The cholent kugel mixture can also be used to stuff calf's intestines, to create the famous *kishke*, or chicken necks.

Serves 6 to 8.

◆ *All the*

ingredients

for a fine

cholent.

SEPHARDIC CHOLENT

A layered hotpot of beans, meat, potatoes
and eggs

12 medium potatoes
2 tablespoons salt
1 lb/450g dry lima/butter beans
salt and pepper
4 large onions, finely chopped
3 tablespoons vegetable oil
1 - 2 lbs/0.5-1.0kg beef, cut into slices
2 lbs/1kg calf's foot, cut into slices
3 small onions, unpeeled
10 hard-boiled eggs in their shells

Pare the potatoes and soak them in water, with the 2 tablespoons salt, for 2 hours. Soak the beans in unsalted water for 2 hours, then drain them and season with salt and pepper. In a large deep pan, sauté the onion in the oil. Remove from the heat and add, in layers, first the beans, then the sliced beef and calf's foot, then the unpeeled onions, then the whole, soaked potatoes, and lastly the hard-boiled eggs. Add just enough water to cover all the ingredients. Bring to a boil and simmer briskly, uncovered, for 30 minutes. Then cover the pan and transfer to a very low oven to cook overnight.
Serves 6 to 8.

DFEENA

Beef stew with calf's foot, hard-boiled
eggs, potatoes and pulses. A Morrocan-
Jewish version of *cholent*, eaten on
festive occasions

1 calf's foot
2 large onions, finely chopped
vegetable oil
2 lbs/1kg stewing beef, cubed
6 small potatoes
6 eggs in their shells, well scrubbed
1 1/2-2lbs/350-450g chickpeas or
navy/haricot beans, soaked overnight
2 cloves garlic, crushed
1 teaspoon ground allspice
salt and freshly ground black pepper

Blanch the calf's foot in boiling water and drain. Fry the onions in oil until they are soft and golden.

Put these and the rest of the ingredients into a large ovenproof pot or casserole with a tight-fitting lid. Cover with water, put the lid on, and cook for 1 hour at 375°F/190°C. Then lower the oven temperature to the lowest setting and continue to cook for several hours, or overnight. Serves 6 to 8.

Note: If you are using beans rather than the more traditional chickpeas, do not add salt until the beans are tender - adding it before seems to prevent them softening.

CHICKEN SOUP WITH KNEIDLACH
Traditional Jewish chicken soup
with dumplings

3 lbs/1.5kg chicken, whole or in pieces, with feet
6 cups/1.5 liters water
2 medium onions, peeled
1 small head celery, chopped
4 carrots, scraped and chopped into thick pieces
pinch paprika
salt and pepper
bunch parsley

KNEIDLACH
1 1/2 cups/ 175g matzo flour
1 cup/ 225ml cold water
3 eggs
1 tablespoon oil
salt, black pepper

Immerse the chicken feet in boiling water for a few seconds and remove the outer skin. Then put the chicken or chicken pieces into a large saucepan, with the feet, and add the water and onions. Bring to a boil, then turn down the heat, cover, and simmer gently for 1 hour. Now add the onions, celery, carrots and other ingredients. Continue to simmer, with the lid on, for another 45 minutes or until the chicken is tender. Pour the broth through a strainer, skim off the fat, adjust the seasoning and return the vegetables to the soup. The chicken can be used for salad or served separately, cut up, with the soup.

To make the *kneidlach*, knead all the ingredients to a smooth dough, cover, and refrigerate overnight. Boil 1 gallon/3 liters water to which 2 tablespoons salt have been added. Roll the dough into balls the size of ping pong balls and cook in the boiling water for 30 minutes - use a slotted spoon to slide them in. Leave the *kneidlach* in the water, keeping hot, until you are ready to serve.

A bowl of grandma's chicken soup is always welcome, but instead of *kneidlach* you could add boiled rice, vermicelli, blanched vegetables or homemade soup checks (see recipe below).

SOUP CHECKS

pinch salt
1 tablespoon oil
4 eggs, well beaten
all-purpose/plain flour
oil for deep frying

Whip/whisk the salt and oil into the eggs, then add flour a tablespoon at a time until you have a soft, smooth dough - don't add too much flour or the dough will be too dry. Roll out the dough on a floured surface until it is pasta-thin. Cut into strips, then into squares of uniform size. Heat the oil. Fry a few squares at a time until they are crisp and golden. Drain on paper towels/kitchen paper. Allow to cool, then store in an airtight container until the grandchildren pay a visit.

◆ *Chicken soup*

with soup

checks,

a marriage

between Jewish

tradition and

Israeli

invention.

KUBBANEH
Steamed sweet rolls

1 oz/25g yeast, fresh or dried
2 tablespoons sugar
1/4 cup/60ml lukewarm water
4 cups and 2 tablespoons/500g all-purpose/plain flour
3/4 tablespoon salt
1 cup/225ml water
2 tablespoons margarine

Combine the yeast, sugar, and water in a small bowl, cover with a clean towel and leave in a warm place for about 10 minutes for the yeast to work.

Sift the flour and the salt into a large mixing bowl, make a well in the middle and pour in the yeast mixture. Knead, gradually adding water, until the dough loses its stickiness. Cover with a towel, put in a warm place and allow to rise for about 15 minutes. Knead again.

Dissolve the margarine in a medium large saucepan which has a tightly fitting lid. Make sure the sides of the saucepan are coated with margarine.

Divide the dough into five portions. Wet your hands and roll each portion into a ball. Put the balls into the saucepan - the margarine will prevent them sticking together. Cover and cook over a very low heat until the balls of dough expand. Now slide an asbestos sheet under the saucepan and continue cooking over a medium low heat until they turn golden yellow and their tops are baked and not sticky. Turn off the heat.

Serve hot, turned upside down. Slice like cake. Serves 5. Serve on Sabbath mornings with *hilbeh* and *haminados* (see recipes pp. 119 and 154).

SENIYEH
A traditional Arab dish of ground meat and *tahini*

8oz/225g ground/minced beef, lamb or veal
2 tablespoons chopped parsley
2 tablespoons finely chopped onion
1 tablespoon flour
1 tablespoon vegetable oil
1/2 teaspoon zhoug (see recipe p. 39)
1/2 teaspoon salt
1/2 teaspoon pepper
2 tablepoons tahini paste
1 tablespoon lemon juice
2 tablespoons water
pine nuts, to garnish

Combine the meat with the vegetables, flour, oil, *zhoug*, salt and pepper, and press into a small, round ovenproof dish. Pre-heat the oven to 350°F/180°C.

With a fork, beat together the *tahini* paste, lemon juice and water, pour over the meat mixture and sprinkle with pine nuts. Bake for 30 minutes. Serve with salad and pickles. Serves 4.

◆ *Yemenite kubbaneh with brown eggs (haminados) and hilbeh. Kubbaneh are eaten for breakfast. Hilbeh is a relish made from fenugreek seeds.*

MEJADARRA
Galilean Arab lentil and rice pilaf

*1 lb/450g large brown lentils, soaked if
necessary
1 onion, finely chopped
3 tablespoons vegetable oil
salt and freshly ground black pepper
8 oz/225g long-grain rice, washed
1 cup/225ml water
2 onions, sliced into half-moon shapes*

Generously cover the lentils with cold water and simmer until tender, removing any scum that rises and adding more water as necessary. Fry the chopped onion in half the oil until soft and golden, then add to the cooked lentils. Season with salt and pepper.

Add the rice and the extra cup of water to the lentils, cover, and simmer gently for about 20 minutes or until the rice is soft. If the rice absorbs the water too quickly, add a little more.

Fry the sliced onions in the rest of the oil until they are dark brown. Heap the rice and lentils onto a warm serving dish and garnish with the caramelized onions.

Mejadarra can be served hot or cold, with fresh yogurt. Serves 5 or 6.

◆ *Mejadarra,*

a classic

vegetarian

combination

of legumes

and rice,

served with

fresh yogurt.

NEW WAVE CHICKEN
Chef I. Nicolai was the father of professional cooking in Israel. This recipe, created in 1950, is typical of his work and of the style he founded.

*1 chicken, weighing 3 lbs/1.5kg, cut into joints
1/2 cup/100g flour
5 tablespoons vegetable oil
1 cup/100g olives, pitted/stoned
12 cloves garlic, peeled
1 small head celery, diced
1/2 teaspoon black peppercorns
1 teaspoon dried tarragon
4 tomatoes, cut into quarters
salt
pinch ground ginger
3 tablespoons cognac
1/2 cup/100ml white wine
3 oranges, sliced fine*

Dip the chicken joints in the flour and shake off the excess. In a large skillet/frying pan heat the oil and fry the joints, turning them occasionally so that they lightly brown on all sides.

Boil 2 cups/450ml water in a small saucepan and add the olives; bring to a boil, then drain and reserve the olives. Blanch 11 of the cloves of garlic in the same way, allowing them to boil for 3 minutes before draining them. Crush the other clove of garlic.

Add all the garlic, olives, celery, peppercorns, tarragon, tomatoes, salt and ginger to the skillet and continue frying for 30 minutes. Now add the sliced oranges. Heat the wine and cognac in a small saucepan, pour over the chicken and set a match to it. Serve immediately with fresh salad, brown bread and fruity white wine. Serves 4.

◆ *A version*

of chicken

with olives,

tarragon and

cognac.

KUGEL

Savoury noodle pudding traditional among Eastern European Jews

8 oz/225g thin vermicelli
1/2 cup/100ml vegetable oil
1/2 cup/100g sugar
salt
1 1/2 teaspoons freshly ground black pepper
3 eggs, lightly beaten

Preheat the oven to 350°F/180°C. Cook the vermicelli in salted water until it is tender, then drain well and set aside. In a medium saucepan, heat the oil and add the sugar. Cook over a very low heat, stirring constantly, for about 10 minutes or until the mixture turns very dark, almost black. Immediately stir in the spaghetti, salt, pepper and beaten eggs. Taste to see if the mixture is peppery enough. If not, add more pepper. Place in a greased tube pan and bake, uncovered, for at least 1 1/2 hours, or until golden brown on top.

Remove the kugel from the oven and unmold it by turning it upside down on a plate. Serve slices with meat, salad or pickles. Other versions with raisins, onions or both are also popular, traditionally served after *cholent*.

◆ *Kugel*

in a pot,

waiting

its turn

after the

cholent.

HILBEH

Fenugreek relish, an exotic addition to soups, excellent for health and stamina

2 tablespoons ground fenugreek seeds
1 fresh tomato, cut into quarters
1/2 teaspoon freshly ground black pepper
2 teaspoons zhoug *(see recipe p. 39)*

Soak the *zhoug* in cold water for 2 hours, then pour off excess water. Using a blender, mix all the other ingredients together, then whip/whisk until fluffy.

◆ *Kugel*

served with

pickles.

VEGETABLES

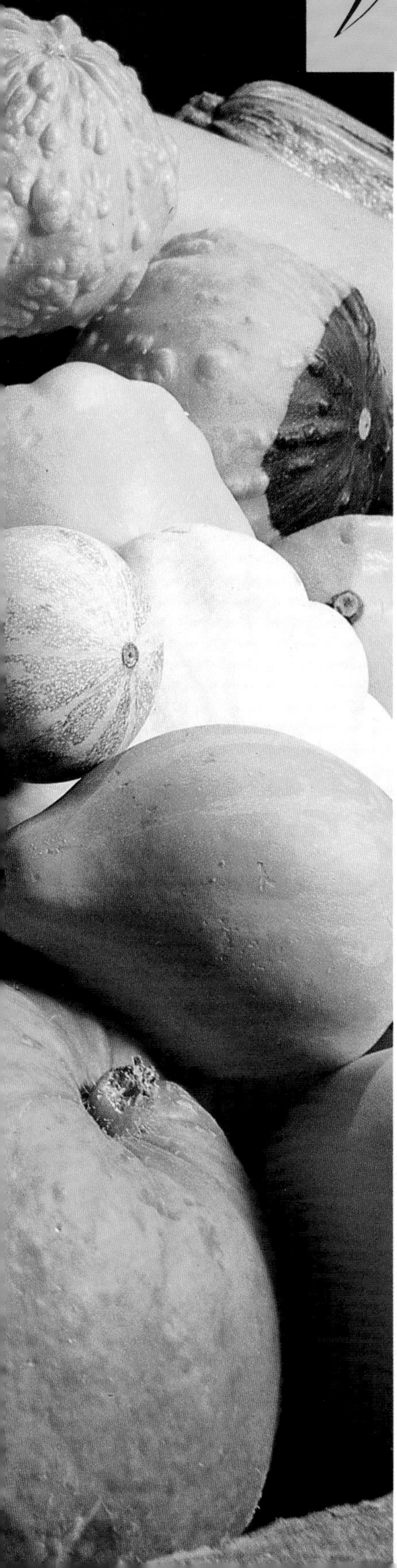

◆A colorful

display of

summer

and winter

squash.

To city-dwelling Israelis, in Jerusalem, Tel Aviv and Haifa, working the land is a romantic, even noble occupation. They like to refer to Israel not as plain Israel but as "the land of Israel" as if annexing to

◆ *Corn*

stubble in

the fertile

Hulah Valley,

a mosquito-

infested

marsh before

it was

drained by

the early

settlers.

themselves the romance and nobility of the agricultural way of life. In truth, a very small proportion of Israelis lead this life today. Their lot is the city, an overwhelming density of traffic, and nowhere to park.

To Israel's early settlers agriculture was a necessity. Dreamers were not welcome; they were unproductive. And yet it was the dreamers who saw in an apple not a fruit but a laboratory, not the status quo but a point of departure for bigger, juicier, firmer apples and trees which yielded bigger crops at more convenient times. Advancing the cause of apples for the good of Israel was a long, tedious process, and the same can be said of many other fruits and vegetables. But the result has been that Israel is, and always has been, a driving force in advancing the principles of modern agriculture. Necessity has taught us to achieve better crops from given plots of land.

Many regional fruit and vegetable specialties have endured down to the present time, although few of our regions now enjoy the isolation which made them regions in the first place. Grapes and apples are grown on the Golan, cereals in the Jezreel Valley and the northern Negev, oranges in the Vale of Capernaum, winter vegetables and subtropical fruits in the

Jordan Valley, tomatoes and other salad vegetables in the Judean desert. Today Israel is self-sufficient in vegetables and supplies planeloads of them, out of season, to Western Europe. Many of them are grown in miles and miles of plastic tunnels.

◆ *Most of the country's wheat is grown in the sandy soil of the northern Negev.*

◆ *Jacob Lichansky*

has played a part

in creating the

new Israeli cuisine.

He has an

unfailing sense

of humor and a

deep understanding

of vegetables and

fish.

◆ *At the experi-*

mental farm of

Neve Yaar, where

new vegetables

and fruits are

coaxed from the

soil - dwarf sweet

corn of various

colors and mini-

watermelons

without seeds.

◆ *Kaspi is a*

local grower who

supplies the hotel

and restaurant

trade. He delivers

everything from

fresh quail eggs

to ripe pine-

apples.

◆ *Shimon Shalvi of*

Nahalal holds the

record for the

largest radish ever

grown in Israel.

He refuses to

reveal his secret.

His pickles are as

incredible as his

radishes.

Thrown in among local Arab communities, with few if any utensils brought from their countries of origin, the early settlers had no choice but to adapt to local conditions. They dug clay ovens in the ground, as the Arabs did. They churned their own butter, and drank the buttermilk. They discovered which vegetables grew and which did not. They made wine out of peaches, apricots and plums. It was a vast learning experience, but its aim was survival, not self-education. They ate what they raised, and they raised what they ate. If they discovered that you get a stronger, more durable orange tree by crossing it with a lemon, they went ahead and crossed it. Their victories were hard-fought and hard-won, and they resented citification and the different morality that it represented.

Longevity is one of the attributes of those who have devoted their lives to inventive farm work. We, or rather the kibbutzim or moshavim in which they live, do not generally allow such people to ease off until they reach their seventies or eighties. Our long-lived, patient, persevering agriculturalists have adapted papayas to regions they were not meant to grow in; perfected new shapes and sizes and flavors of apples (and often named them after their grand-

◆ *Freshly pressed olive oil is checked for color, aroma and consistency. The right blend of green and black olives yields the desired quality.*

◆ *During the olive harvest the entire village of Mrar is busy with olive oil production.*

daughters); introduced celery, broccoli, brussels sprouts and Chinese cabbage to a country that was perfectly happy with ordinary cabbages, potatoes and onions; pioneered the spaghetti squash, a peculiar melon-shaped fruit that disintegrates into noodles when you cook it; taken the thorns off prickly pears, and in the process rather modified our thorny image of ourselves; and done everything possible to ensure that seasonal produce matures on a precise day, at a precise hour, in order to hit the market at precisely the right moment.

It may sound surprising, but in a country known for the quantity and quality of its fruits and vegetables, the use of fresh herbs is only just beginning to catch on. Various ethnic groups have always used coriander and mint, but until recently neither of these herbs was grown commercially. Fresh herbs such as parsley, basil, oregano, tarragon, chives and sage are now available at most good produce stores, although they are still viewed with some suspicion. Nevertheless the appearance of a range of fresh herbs is a clear signal that a new culinary age has dawned. They suggest that hamburgers and processed foods may be in retreat.

◆ *Tomatoes are sorted according to size and quality before they are crated and shipped.*

$\mathscr{V}$EGETABLES

◆ *Israeli salad is an adaptation of an earlier Arab dish.*

Recipes

AVOCADO WITH TAHINI YOGURT

1 cup/225ml plain yogurt
1/3 cup/80ml tahini paste
1/2 teaspoon ground cumin
pinch ground coriander
1/4 teaspoon finely chopped garlic
1 tablespoon lemon juice
1/4 teaspoon salt
1/4 teaspoon pepper
pinch cayenne pepper
3 ripe avocadoes
1/2 cup/100g flaked almonds, toasted

Beat the yogurt into the *tahini*, then add the spices, herbs, and seasonings. Blend well, cover and refrigerate. Peel the avocados a few minutes before serving, halving them lengthwise and removing the pits/stones. Thinly slice each half lengthwise and fan out the slices on individual plates. Spoon the yogurt dressing over them and sprinkle with toasted almonds. Serves 6.

Note: When preparing avocados, squeeze a little lemon juice into a bowl of water and dip the avocados into it as you peel or slice them. This will prevent the flesh turning an unappetizing grey-black.

AVOCADO & POMEGRANATE SALAD

2 ripe avocados
1 pomegranate
4 oz/100g black grapes
lemon juice
water

DRESSING
1 teaspoon sugar
4 tablespoons white wine vinegar
2 tablespoons corn oil
1 tablespoon groundnut oil
4 tablespoons chopped mint
salt and pepper

Peel the avocados, remove the pits/stones, and slice into thick half rings. Drop the rings into a bowl containing water and lemon juice–this will prevent them turning black.

Cut the pomegranate in half and crush it over a bowl to remove and collect the seeds. Wash the grapes and mix them with the pomegranate seeds. Drain the avocado pieces and add them to the fruit.

To make the dressing, put all the ingredients into a glass jar, screw the lid on firmly and shake vigorously for 2 minutes. Pour over the avocado and fruit. Toss well before serving. Serves 4 to 6.

◆ *Avocado and pomegranate salad. Israel and the avocado are almost synonymous. In fact avocados have now outstripped oranges as our top export .*

FRIED EGGPLANT SALAD

2 lbs/900g eggplants/aubergines
2 tablespoons coarse salt
1 cup/100g flour
oil for deep frying
1/2 cup/100ml white vinegar
4 oz/100g chili peppers, assorted colors, seeded
and finely sliced
6 cloves garlic, finely chopped
2 or 3 tablespoons water

Cut the eggplants, unpeeled, into slices 1/2 inch/1cm thick. Put them in a colander and sprinkle them with salt. Leave for 30 minutes to drain, then squeeze out excess moisture. Dust the pieces sparingly with flour and deep-fry in hot oil.

In a large bowl, mix the vinegar with the chili peppers and garlic, and add 2 or 3 tablespoons of water. Add the hot slices of eggplant and mix gently. Allow to cool, then pack into glass jars, seal and refrigerate. This salad can be eaten freshly made, but it improves with keeping.

◆ *Spaghetti*

squash with

eggplant &

sesame.

SPAGETTI SQUASH WITH EGGPLANT & SESAME

1 large eggplant/aubergine
3 tablespoons olive oil
3 lbs/1.5kg cooked spaghetti squash
1/2 cup/100g sesame seeds
2 tablespoons butter
3 cloves garlic, minced
salt and pepper to taste
1 cup/100g grated Parmesan cheese

Pre-heat oven to 450°F/230°C. Top and tail the eggplant, cut it into 8 slices lengthwise and sprinkle with salt. Allow to drain for 20 minutes, then squeeze out excess moisture and pat dry. Brush with olive oil and place, in a single layer, on a baking sheet. Bake for 15-20 minutes or until the slices begin to soften.

To prepare the spaghetti squash, cut the squash in half, discard the seeds, and boil for about 20 minutes. Rinse under cold water to loosen the "spaghetti" and drain well. Lightly toast the sesame seeds, taking care not to let them singe. Dip the eggplant slices in the seeds, then roll them up with a spoonful of Parmesan inside. Heat the butter in a large skillet/frying pan and fry the garlic for 2 minutes. Carefully stir in the spaghetti squash, season with salt and pepper, and add the rest of the Parmesan.

Transfer to a warm serving dish, arrange the rolled eggplant slices on top and serve immediately.

◆ *Spaghetti*

squash

undergoing

further

development

at Neve Yaar.

MEDITERRANEAN SALAD

6 tablespoons olive oil
1 large clove garlic, minced
1 teaspoon cumin seeds, crushed
1/4 cup/60ml fresh lemon juice
4 large tomatoes, cut into wedges, then halved
2 medium zucchini/courgettes, sliced into thin rounds
2 medium green bell peppers, cut into bite size squares
2 small onions, chopped
4 oz/100g black olives, pitted
4 tablespoons chopped parsley
salt and freshly ground black pepper

Heat the oil in a large, heavy skillet/frying pan, but do not allow it to smoke. Add the garlic and cumin and fry for 2 minutes until the cumin releases its fragrance. Remove from the heat and cool to room temperature. Stir in the lemon juice.

Combine the tomatoes, zucchini, peppers, onions, olives and parsley in a large bowl. Add the dressing and toss well. Season with salt and pepper. Cover and refrigerate. Serve chilled. Serves 12.

◆ *An old olive press in the Druze village of Mrar.*

ISRAELI SALAD

For this you need good vegetables, good olive oil and the ability to enjoy the simple things in life.

2 large tomatoes
2 cucumbers
1 large onion
4 tablespoons finely chopped parsley
1/2 lemon
1/4 cup/60 ml superb olive oil
salt and black pepper to taste
chopped fresh mint, optional

Dice the vegetables with a very sharp knife - they should be cut very small and evenly. Red cabbage, green bell pepper or garlic can be added to the standard recipe given above, but only one deviation is allowed at a time! Squeeze and strain the lemon juice over the vegetables, then add the other ingredients. Toss well before serving.

PICKLED CUCUMBERS

2-4 lbs/0.9-1.8kg baby cucumbers
fresh dill
10 cloves garlic
sea salt
water

Put a sprig or two of dill and 4 or 5 cloves of garlic in the bottom of a large glass jar, then pack the cucumbers on top. Cover with water, measuring it into the jar. For each cup/225ml of water added, add 1 tablespoon sea salt. Add more dill and cloves of garlic, then seal. Put the jar in the sun so that the cucumbers change color.

EGGPLANT STUFFED WITH MUSHROOMS & OLIVES

2 eggplants/aubergines
1 tablespoon salt
1 tablespoon vegetable oil
1 cup/150g olives, pitted/stoned
2 onions, sliced
1 bell pepper, cut into strips
12 oz/350g baby mushrooms
3 tablespoons fresh lemon juice
3 tablespoons olive oil
2 cloves garlic, crushed
2 tablespoon chopped dill
2 tablespoon wine vinegar

Pre-heat the oven to 375°F/190°C. Cut the eggplants in half lengthwise, sprinkle with salt, and leave to drain for 20 minutes. Squeeze out the excess moisture, then place on an oiled baking sheet. Bake until they are fairly soft, then scoop out some of the flesh and reserve.

Meanwhile, boil up a little water and blanch the olives in it - do this twice to remove their saltiness. Lightly fry the onions in the vegetable oil, remove the skillet/ frying pan from the heat and add the pepper strips, mushrooms, lemon juice, olive oil, garlic and vinegar. Mix well together. Mash the scooped out eggplant and add to the mixture. Divide the mixture between the four eggplant halves and put them back in the oven for 10 minutes.

Serve sprinkled with dill, accompanied by a yogurt-based sauce.

PICKLED BELL PEPPERS

1 1/2 lbs/700g green bell peppers
1 1/2 lbs/700g red bell peppers
2 1/2 cups/600ml distilled white vinegar
1 1/4 cups/275g sugar
2 1/2 cups/600ml water
8 cloves garlic
4 teaspoons vegetable oil
2 teaspoons salt
4 sprigs dill

Remove the stems and seeds from the peppers and cut into 2-inch/5-cm wide strips. Put the strips into a large bowl, cover with boiling water and allow to stand for 5 minutes. Drain well, then pack the strips into 4 pint-sized (450ml) sterilized jars, adding 2 cloves of garlic, a teaspoon of oil, a sprig of dill and 1/2 teaspoon of salt to each jar.

In a stainless steel or enamel saucepan, combine the vinegar, sugar and water, and bring to a boil. Ladle this mixture into the jars, filling them to within 1/4 inch/0.5cm of the top. Wipe the tops of the jars with a damp cloth and put the lids on.

Place the jars in a deep saucepan with a rack in the bottom and add enough water to cover the jars by 2 inches/5 cms. Bring the water to a boil and boil for 5 minutes. Remove the jars from the saucepan with tongs and allow them to cool. Store in a cool, dark place.

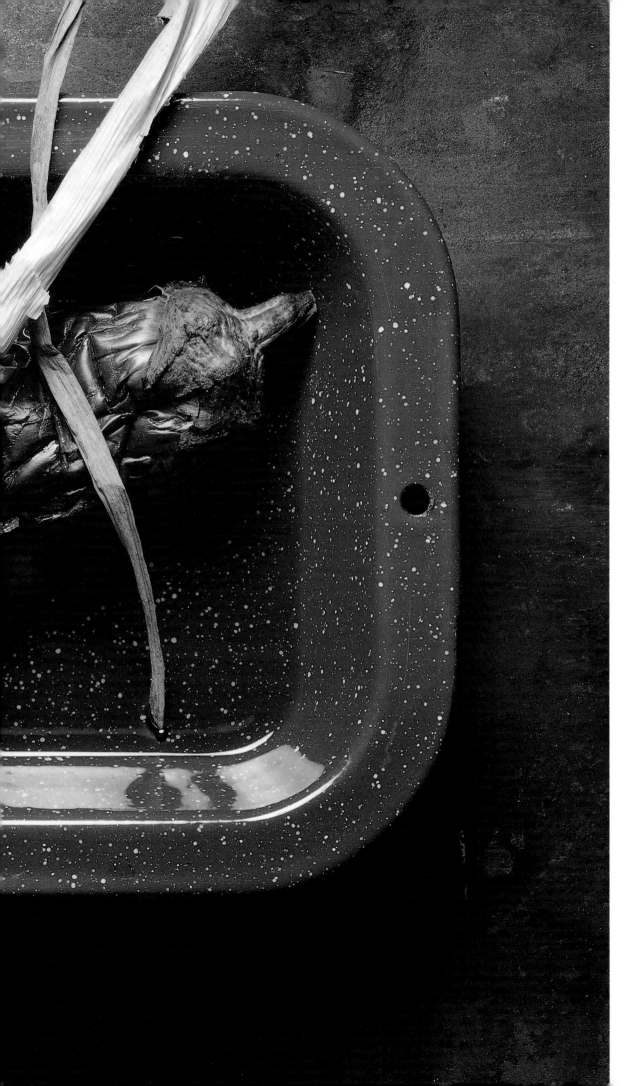

◆ *Eggplant*

and garlic

could be the

cure to many

of the great

problems of

our time.

STUFFED VEGETABLES

Stuffed vegetables, as a starter or a main course, are the pride of everyone who serves them. They are very Mediterranean, whether baked, poached or gently stewed in a tomato sauce. The stuffing in the next recipe is a typical one, but it can be varied by adding liver or pine nuts, or by using lamb instead of beef. If you are stuffing eggplants, remember to salt and drain them first.

◆ *Assorted*

stuffed

vegetables -

onion,

zucchini,

eggplant,

and red

pepper.

◆ *Eggplant*

stuffed with

mushrooms,

olives, red

pepper and

onion.

STUFFED ONIONS

2 large onions
2 oz/60g butter
water
2 tablespoons lemon or lime juice

STUFFING
8 oz/225 lean beef, ground/minced
3 oz/80g rice, washed thoroughly and drained
2 tablespoons finely chopped parsley
1 teaspoon salt
1/2 teaspoon black pepper
1/2 teaspoon ground allspice

Peel the onions. With a sharp knife, make a cut in each one from top to bottom on one side, cutting toward the center. Cook the onions in boiling water for about 45 minutes or until the layers detach easily. Drain and leave until cool enough to handle.

Meanwhile, knead together all the stuffing ingredients to a smooth, well blended consistency.

Carefully separate the layers of onion. Into the hollow of each layer put 1 tablespoon of stuffing, more for the outer layers, less for the inner. Roll up each layer into a little parcel and tie with a piece of thread. Pre-heat the oven to 350°F/180°C.

Melt the butter in a skillet/frying pan and sauté the onion parcels, a few at a time, turning occasionally, until they are a light golden color. When all the parcels have been sautéed, pack them tightly into an shallow oiled ovenproof dish and pour in just enough boiling water to cover them by 1/2-inch/1cm or so. Sprinkle with the lemon or lime juice and cover.

Bake in the oven for about 1 hour or until the meat is cooked. Serve with fresh salad or boiled potatoes. Serves 4 to 6.

STREET FOOD

◆ Falafel
fried in the
traditional
manner.
The patties
are shaped
with a special
implement
which is also
used to slip
them into the
hot oil.

A lot of eating out in Israel is done standing up. The sit-down restaurant-type meal has only recently evolved, for in many ways we are still an eat-it-while-you-can society. We are obsessive, short-tempered, driven, on the move. We have a need to consume quickly, to eat and run. Leisure is not part of the Israeli lifestyle.

Nothing more clearly reveals this fact than the roaring trade done by restaurants and snack stands at gas stations. Most countries provide food and refreshment at gas stations, usually of the franchised, fast-food variety, but in Israel roadside culinary attractions are more ambitious. While the tank is being filled and the oil is being checked, you are invited to consume - quickly of course - a sample of *mezze*, grilled meat or fish, or something in the dessert line. The quality is comparable to that of most average restaurants serving similar food. Do not expect gourmet. Do not expect fancy. When you stop in the middle of the desert on your way to Eilat, do not think *haute cuisine*. Think adequate. And you will be pleasantly surprised.

◆ Mezze *are calculated to make gourmands of the most dedicated gourmets!*

Gas station dining is now such an institution that we eat in gas stations even when we are not in the car. We walk there, treading gingerly around the oil slicks and gas puddles. We sit down. We order off a paper napkin or off the wall. And the food arrives at a furious pace, whole trayfuls of it. Could we survive without *pita* bread? Probably not. Here it is, any way you want it - warmed over, grilled to a crispy cracker, cut open and toasted. Here comes the *mezze* selection - a dozen small plates of dips and salads and pickles. As the pumps ring, we scoop up their colorful contents with our *pita* bread. Knives and forks only slow you down. Sweet Turkish coffee to finish. With the last gulp, we move off. We do not linger. Traffic continues to pour in.

◆ *Turko is a*
borekas
vendor in
HaCarmel
market.
He fills his
borekas with
whatever his
customers
want.

When leisure is not a part of life, food tends to be consumed rather than enjoyed, and Israel is not noted for its leisure time. So far, the need to eat and run has found many admirable solutions. Perhaps, when we slow down a bit, we will be less rough and ready, but never more colorful.

Pedestrians are exposed to other kinds of street food. The king - by popular consent - is *falafel*, fried patties made from chickpeas, herbs and spices crammed into *pita* bread with salads and relishes. Israel has contributed much to the course of *falafel*. It was here, ready and waiting, when we needed a national food. A newly created state, a toddler nation, what were we to eat that we could call our own? *Falafel*. It mattered little that *falafel* was an Arab invention, that it had existed longer than Israel and Israelis. We needed something, and *falafel* was it. Nutritious, tasty, spicy, quick and easy to prepare and plentiful at street corners. Colorful, photogenic *falafel* stands, manned by boisterous, aggressive vendors stuffing half or whole pockets of *pita* bread full to bursting with hot, round, fragrant patties, various salads and deep-fried potatoes dipped in batter - what could be better? The whole package was then handed to the customer, who proceeded to add the condiments of his choice from an array of large containers on a tray. All-round favorites were *harissa* (hot pepper paste) and *tahini* (savoury sesame seed paste), watery and diluted so that they trickled and flowed through the contents of the *pita* pocket, down your arm and into your sleeve...You ate leaning forward slightly, so that whatever dropped did not stain your shirt or land on your shoes.

That was then. In those days *falafel* was judged by its texture and taste, by the way the crushed chickpeas yielded to the teeth, by whether it was mild and restrained - the tamed Ashkenazi variety - or hot and spicy - the genuine Sephardic kind. The salads had to be fresh, the *pita* warm from the oven, the condiments fiery, aggressive and reeking of cumin.

145

That has all gone now. If you search hard, in Arab villages and along country roads, you may still stumble on an old-fashioned *falafel* stand. But you have to know where to look, and when you get there it may have disappeared. Today's *falafel* joints are huge hangars in which all the components are laid out like the ammunition of a fighter plane. Today *falafel* is about quantity, not

quality. Competition is fierce. Arab vendors, who prepare better *falafel* than anyone else, are confined to their own trading areas.

For the price of one *falafel*, you are allowed any number of refills, so really the *pita* pocket is all you pay for. We seem to have devised a way of having our *falafel* and eating it. But there is something demeaning about the free *falafel* economy. The sky-high piles of pickled cabbage and salad and assorted pickles, and the precariously balanced heaps of cold patties, are hardly inviting. Street food should be sensual, oily, noisy and satisfying. But by encouraging us to pig out on multiple, self-served refills, the *falafel* industry has set back the cause of street food. I want my *falafel* man to fill my *pita* himself. He knows his patties, his salads and his hot stuffs. As he assembles the package, he signs it with a seal of quality. He is a proud craftsman. He would not sell me cold patties or stale potatoes. By removing *falafel* from his supervision, we rob him of his art.

Which brings me to the lynchpin and sine qua non of the *falafel*, the *pita*. Whatever you do with a *pita*, it is always a meal. Even when we eat at a table, we Israelis would rather have our food in a *pita* than on a plate. The small *pita* is the most common, but a larger one, commonly called the Iraqi *pita* since

◆ *Jerusalem mixed grill is a whole meal in a* pita. *Chicken spleens, livers, hearts and spices are some of the ingredients.*

146

it was introduced by Iraqi Jews, is also popular. It does not have a pocket, so its role is limited to scooping up *hummus* and similar delicacies, and wrapping. There is a suburb of Tel Aviv, well known for its culinary offerings, which is big on Iraqi *pita*. When you order your favorite meal on a skewer, the grill man will place your skewer on a hot Iraqi *pita*, fold it once and pull the skewer expertly out, leaving the meat in place. He then opens the *pita*,

adds *tahini* or *harissa*, a salad or french fries, and refolds it in such a manner that it will not leak or break as you eat it. Folding an Iraqi *pita* is an art in itself.

The Tunisian answer to *falafel* is the *brik*, a crusty little triangle of *filo* dough filled with cheese or potato. In fact the *brik* is a cousin of the larger *boreka*, which plays a strong second to *falafel*. Today *borekas* are mass produced and franchised by a central bakery, but not so long ago vendors would fill a *boreka* in front of your very eyes and offer vegetables and a brown egg with it.

A lot of our street food moves. Since Israel is a small country and mostly flat, you can cover it quite easily with a pushcart. Fruit and vegetables, especially watermelons, are sold from the back of horse-drawn carts. Step out in your pajamas to meet the roving watermelon man! But gone are the days when small carts pushed by children brought prickly pears to the door. We used to buy them already peeled and almost thornless and eat them then and there.

Warm local bagels are still sold on street corners, but there are few vendors today who will freely and happily give you their home-mixed *za'atar*, a salty mixture of spices, hyssop and other herbs. They hide it and you have to ask for it. But once upon a time little cornets of *za'atar* done up in newspaper were openly displayed and you helped yourself. You dipped your chewy bagel into the *za'atar* between each bite.

A combination of the Israeli sweet tooth and the hot, humid climate is chiefly responsible for two other street food relics: the *tamarindi* seller and the *malabi* cart. *Tamarindi* is a sweet, syrupy beverage derived from the tamarind fruit and it is poured from a jar carried on the vendor's shoulder. *Malabi* is a dessert, a white, caramel-like custard sold in small tin cups. Since the mixture is practically tasteless, it is sold with a choice of syrups. You select a syrup flavor and the vendor splashes a generous amount of it into the little cup and hands it to you with a spoon. His little cart is totally self-contained catering unit. It has a bed of ice for the *malabi* to stand in, and a small water tank and faucet for washing out the empty cups. More than any other form of street food, the *malabi* cart is a magnet for a strange mixture of clients. Hurrying mechanics and well-groomed businessmen flock around it, happily absorbing the contents of the little cups. *Malabi* is hardly food. It does not nourish or allay hunger. It is a dessert through and through. You only eat it because you are addicted to it.

◆ *A large Iraqi pita used to wrap a kebab, hummus, mango chutney and cabbage.*

$\mathscr{S}$ TREET FOOD

Recipes

FALAFEL

1 cup/225g dried chickpeas
5 cups/1.2 liters water
1 teaspoon baking soda
1 teaspoon salt
1 teaspoon cumin seeds
1 teaspoon coriander
1 onion, quartered
2 tablespoons minced parsley
2 cloves garlic, mashed
freshly ground black pepper
1 tablespoon lemon juice
pinch chili pepper
vegetable oil for deep frying

Soak the chickpeas in the water for 24 hours, then drain them and put them and all the other ingredients, except the oil, through a meat grinder, twice. Mix together lightly with a fork. The mixture should be loose and crumbly.

Pour 2 inches/5cm of oil into a wok or other utensil for deep frying and set over a medium low heat; the oil should be 350-375°F/180 -190°C when you put the *falafel* in.

While the oil is heating, shape the first batch of patties. Use a generous spoonful of mixture for each patty and don't be too neat about the shaping. Because the mixture is crumbly, it will only just hold together. Each patty should be about 2 1/2 inches/6cm across and 3/4 inch/2cm thick in the middle. Slide the first batch of patties into the hot oil and fry for about 4 minutes, turning at least once. Remove with a slotted spoon and drain on paper towels/kitchen paper. Repeat until all the mixture is used up. Serve as a *mezze* dish, or in *pita* bread with salads, *zhoug*, *tahini* and more.

JERUSALEM MIXED GRILL

4 oz/100g chicken livers
4 oz/100g chicken hearts
2 oz/60g chicken spleens
2 oz/60g turkey fries, optional
2 tablespoons oil
1 onion, sliced
3 cloves garlic, chopped
1/2 teaspoon each of salt, ground cumin,
coriander and turmeric
2 pitas, halved and warmed

Jerusalem mixed grill is not grilled but fried! Cut the livers into small pieces, and halve the hearts and spleens. Using a heavy skillet/frying pan, heat the oil and sweat the slices of onion. Add the garlic, salt and spices, and fry gently until the meat is tender. Serve in *pitas*, perhaps with a lacing of *hummus* (see recipe p. 39). Real gourmets make their mixed grills with pigeon livers, hearts, etc.

◆ Falafel *stands*

are shrines of

creativity.

You pay for a

pita *and you*

assemble your

own filling.

Pickles, zhoug

and tahini *are a*

must.

CHEESE OR SPINACH BOREKAS

8 oz/225g filo *pastry*
2/3 cup/150g melted butter
1 egg yolk, beaten with 1 tablespoon water,
to glaze
sesame seeds, to garnish

CHEESE FILLING
1/2 cup/100g soft white cheese
1 cup/225g finely grated Gruyère
2 tablespoons cream cheese
1 large or 2 small eggs, lightly beaten
salt and pepper

SPINACH FILLING
1 lb/450g fresh spinach
1 egg, lightly beaten
1 cup/225g finely grated Gruyère
salt and pepper

Remove the *filo* leaves from the refrigerator 2 hours before you need them.

To make the cheese filling, simply mash all the ingredients together with a fork or combine them in a food processor.

To make the spinach filling, wash the spinach several times, put the wet leaves into a saucepan without any extra water, cover tightly and sweat over a medium heat for 4 or 5 minutes until tender. Drain in a sieve, pressing out any excess moisture. Chop fine and combine with the egg, cheese, salt and pepper.

Pre-heat the oven to 350°F/180°C.

Taking one leaf of *filo* at a time, cut it into a strip about 6 inches/15cm wide by 12 inches/30cm long and brush with melted butter. Now fold it in half so that it is the same length but half the width. Brush with butter again. Place a heaped tablespoon of cheese or spinach filling at one end, and fold the end over to make a triangle. Butter the top of the triangle, then fold over again. Continue until the entire strip is folded into a triangle, brushing with butter between each folding. Put the completed triangles onto a greased baking sheet and brush the tops with egg yolk and water to glaze. Sprinkle with sesame seeds.

Bake for 25-30 minutes, until golden brown and puffy. Serve warm or cold, but not hot.

Borekas can also be made with puff pastry. Just fold the pastry over the fillings and proceed as above. Although baking is the traditional method of cooking borekas, many street vendors deep-fry them. The shape of a boreka usually tells you what the filling is - triangles for cheese, squares for potatoes, twists for spinach.

◆*Assorted*

borekas with

brown eggs

(haminados).

The fillings vary

from cheese

through spinach

to potato.

GREEN OMELET

2 eggs per person
2 tablespoons water
1 tablespoon oil, or oil and butter together
2 tablespoons finely chopped parsley
1 tablespoon finely chopped coriander
1 tablespoon finely chopped dill
2 tablespoons finely chopped watercress,
optional
salt and black pepper
pinch cumin

This can be cooked with the greenery beaten into the eggs or spread on top of the finished article.

Beat the eggs and water together first. Heat the oil in a skillet/frying pan, make sure it is really hot, then swiftly cook two very thin omelets, turning them so that they cook on both sides. Serve in a brown bread roll with lettuce and a few slices of tomato.

HAMINADOS
Brown eggs

12 eggs
skins of 2 lbs/1kg onions
1 tablespoon flour

Put the eggs in a casserole of cold water, with the onion skins. Bring to a boil and cook for 30 minutes. Mix the flour with a little water, smear the mixture around the rim of the casserole, put the lid on, and put in a very low oven - 120°F/45°C - overnight. The flour makes a perfect seal. Serve with *borekas* and *hummus*.

◆ Borekas

served with

drinking

yogurt and

a brown

egg.

FRIED KIBBEH
Lamb and cracked wheat patties

1 1/2 cups/350g fine bulgur wheat/
cracked wheat
8 oz/225g lean lamb, minced three times
1 onion, minced
3/4 teaspoon curry powder
1/4 teaspoon ground allspice
1/4 teaspoon ground cinnamon
1/4 teaspoon paprika or cayenne
salt and pepper
1/4 cup/60ml olive oil

FILLING
8oz/225g ground/minced meat
3 tablespoons water
1 onion, chopped
2 tablespoons oil
1 teaspoon pine nuts, optional
black pepper and salt to taste
pinch allspice and cinnamon

Soak the bulgur in cold water for 10 minutes, then drain in a fine sieve and squeeze out the excess moisture.

Now combine the lamb, onion, curry powder, allspice, cinnamon, paprika or cayenne, salt and pepper with the soaked bulgur and knead to a smooth, even consistency (if you moisten your hands occasionally, the mixture will not stick to them).

To make the filling, knead the meat and water together, fry the onions in the oil until golden brown, then add the meat and the rest of the ingredients. Fry until fairly dry and crumbly. Chill.

Now form the bulgur mixture into sausages 4 inches/10cm long, and make a hollow in the middle with your finger - wet your finger so that the mixture does not stick. Fill the hollows with the crumbly meat mixture, and pinch the ends together.

(cont'd next page)

Heat the oil in a large, heavy skillet/frying pan until it is hot but not smoking, and fry the *kibbeh* for 3 or 4 minutes on each side or until they begin to color. Transfer them to a warm serving dish with a slotted spoon. Serves 6.

TUNISIAN SANDWICH

4 lemons
1 tablespoon coarse salt
1/2 teaspoon turmeric
2 potatoes
4 long brown loaves or 2 small baguettes
harissa *(see recipe p. 41)*
1 tomato, diced
1 cucumber, diced
1 onion, finely chopped
2 tablespoons capers
8 oz/225g canned tuna
4 oz/100g black olives

At the sandwich stand, they always seem to work very slowly, considering deeply such matters as proportion, tactics and the order of things. This is what sandwich selling is all about.

First you prepare 3 of the lemons, by slicing them, soaking them in cold water for 5 hours, boiling them, draining them, covering them with water again, adding salt and turmeric, and boiling again. Then you cut each slice into 4 triangles and add the juice of the fourth lemon. Then you boil the potatoes until they are soft, after which you drain and peel them, and cut them into 1/2-inch/1-cm cubes. Now you cut the loaves in half lengthwise, leaving a hinge of crust on one side, spread each half with *harissa* and pile in the lemons, potatoes, vegetables, capers, tuna, olives and lemons again.

◆ *Tunisian sandwich, a "hero sandwich" with an amazing filling.*

BARBECUE

◆ *A leg of*

lamb

roasting

over an

open fire.

Israelis are prepared for two emergencies: army reserve duty and barbecues. The two are not necessarily separate. They may even be complementary. The gear in both cases is very basic. For the first one needs a pair of army boots, a backpack containing the bare necessities, and a licensed gun or pistol. The second requires a miniature hibachi forged from the cheapest tin, a pair of rusty tongs, and a bag of charcoal. Some reservists are more ready than others; some do not even bother to remove their equipment from the trunk of the car. Since emergencies always occur in the middle of the night, it is wiser to keep everything in the car rather than clang down the stairs at dawn.

Simple equipment has a lot to recommend it. It is the stripped down, modest approach which is chiefly responsible for the quality of grilled meat. Who needs fancy charcoal - *mesquite*, cherry wood, walnut wood, and so on? Honest charcoal has been made and used in Israel for ages - the largest Arab town, Um-el-Fahem, is named after the stuff. Most Israelis spend their lives within meat-turning distance of an open charcoal grill, but I do not remember a single conversation in which the nature of the charcoal was discussed. Nor do I remember any fancy fire starters. How do we start a grill? The most prevalent method involves heavy use of gasoline. You go into the woods, set up the hibachi, empty a bag of charcoal into it, then douse it liberally with gasoline from the car. You warn the children to stay away, then you throw in a match. The hibachi catches fire with a whoosh that endangers the whole forest, but the conflagration soon dies down and the coals reach the desired state of white glowing ashes. Generations of Israelis have grown up confusing the odour of gasoline with the taste and smell of grilled meat.

On calm windless days we resort to that indispensable tool of the dedicated griller, the fan. Any fan... the back of a broken chair, a piece of card, a magazine. Fanning is an art in itself. You hold your fan and wave, and the frequent gusts of air bring the coals to life. It is not a task to be taken lightly. It requires full attention, a flick of the wrist, a sense of rhythm and timing. Self-igniting charcoal, mostly French, was introduced here recently, but it takes

◆ Our favorite pastime: cooking in the woods. Note the cardboard being used as a fan.

forever to get going, and flickers and hisses gloomily when it does. There is no substitute for a good breeze or a talented fanner.

In Israel, barbecuing is part of the collective memory. It is a national pastime that spares no one, except members of the orthodox community. Twenty years ago, a barbecue was the highlight of a country outing.

Families drove into the hills, children picked wild flowers, mothers spread blankets and fathers got the fire started. Today it is customary to forego the beauty of the scenery and the fresh country air and make do with any grassy knoll. Some Israelis even grill their chops at the grassy intersections of busy streets.

The quality of Israeli meat is steadily improving. One can now ask for and get specific cuts of meat. There are butchers who really know their meat and hang it properly and recommend what cuts to buy. But even though the quality of our meat is better and we have learned to appreciate a good lamb chop, the grills we use allow minimal distance between the rack and the coals.

More than any other facet of Israeli cuisine, grilling meat over an open fire represents an assimilation of Arab tradition with that of Western and Eastern Europe. Most restaurants serving meat offer grilled skewers of meat. Arabs lean more heavily towards lamb, while Jews still prefer lean beef and ground meat. There are exceptions of course. South American Jews know a lot about *carne asado* and *chorizos*, and keep their meat away from open fire, and Jews from North Africa and the Yemen have a cuisine

◆ *Israelis raise geese for their livers.*

◆ *Free-range chickens are catching on.*

which is all their own. But most of the grilled meat consumed in Israel is skewered in cubes on metal spits and quickly cooked over intense heat. Only fancy restaurants comply with requests for rare or medium rare. In most places you are not asked what degree of doneness you require. You get it well done.

"We stole this idea, like so much else, from the Indians," wrote one American food critic, referring to the barbecue. Late in the sixteenth century John White, who was with the settlement on Roanoke Island, Virginia, wrote about the Indians he saw "broyling their fishe over the flame", adding "they took great heed that they bee not burnt." In 1705 Robert Beverly, in *The History and Present State of Virginia*, described the "Indian thing" in a little more detail: "The meat was laid... upon sticks raised upon forks at some distance above the live coals, which heats more gently and dries up the gravy." Two centuries later the United States Department of Agriculture pronounced: "Barbecue is meat that shall be cooked by the direct action of heat resulting from the burning of hard wood or the hot coals therefrom for a sufficient period to assume the usual characteristics...which include the formation of a brown crust." All of these educated essays ignore the Middle East and its humble but considerable contribution to the history of the barbecue. It is difficult to say,

faced with so many conflicting stories, how or where the barbecue came into existence, but my opinion is that it did so 27,000 years ago, within hours of the discovery of fire. The first barbecue writer has to be Homer: "Automedon held the meats and brilliant Achilles carved them, and cut them well into pieces and spitted them."

◆ *Much of the beef raised in Israel ends up sizzling over a grill.*

◆ *Although*

they are no

longer

nomads,

Bedouins

still herd

sheep in the

Negev.

In 1960 James Beard, discussing the changing art of the American barbecue, wrote: "What a phenomenal change! Just twenty years ago when I first wrote about outdoor cooking, backyard chefs were few. And their usual fare was steak or hamburger, blackened in an inferno of smoke and flame." Without wishing to defame a whole nation, it is my sad duty to state that he must have had Israel in mind in that sentence. Unlike cooks in large parts of the rest of the world, Israeli cooks started with the barbecue and advanced backwards to sauces and soufflés.

I grew up knowing more about barbecuing than about any other method of cooking. For many years, going out meant eating grilled meat. Other people went out for hamburgers and pizzas, but we went out for kebabs. They were cheap and satisfying. A kebab is still the cheapest form of cooked meat one can buy. To the suspicious mind, the fact that it costs so little suggests meat of dubious origin. Once upon a time, when you asked for lamb, you got turkey laced with lamb fat, and when you asked for veal, you got chicken. If meat carved from a spit was mysterious, the ground meats used for skewered patties were even more so. But all this is changing. Steaks are usually beef, cut thin. When we come across genuine ground lamb, or cubes of lamb, we know what we are eating. Lamb is the king of kebabs - fragrant, spicy, sometimes spiked with cinnamon, and loaded with chopped parsley and pine nuts.

Considering the years of hostile criticism levelled at grilled meat, it took an amazingly long time for fish to make its way onto the barbecue rack. Mediterranean fish responds well to intense heat and a touch of smoke. Try it once, and you will be converted. The grill leaves gentle marks on the crisp skin and the sea taste is sealed inside. A good, lemony sauce is all the accompaniment it needs. We also have gentler methods of barbecuing fish, in wrappings of vine leaves for instance.

As all food and restaurant guides recommend on those rare occasions when they include Israel: when in Israel, barbecue.

BARBECUE

Recipes

◆ *Spitting*

images:

shish kebab,

skewered

beef marrow,

and lamb

shashlik.

SHASHLIK
Lamb on skewers

MARINADE
1/2 cup/100ml fresh lemon juice
1/2 cup/100ml dry red wine
3 tablespoons chopped fresh rosemary, or
1 tablespoon dried, and
rosemary sprigs to garnish
1 tablespoon finely chopped garlic
1 teaspoon dried hot red pepper flakes
1 1/2 teaspoons salt
3/4 teaspoon freshly ground black pepper
3/4 cup/175ml olive oil

MEAT AND VEGETABLES
leg of lamb weighing 4 lbs/1.8kg, boned and cut
into 2-inch/5-cm cubes
4 medium zucchini/courgettes
4 small onions
4 yellow bell peppers
1 lb/450g cherry tomatoes

Mix together the marinade ingredients, whipping/whisking in the oil in a steady stream so that the mixture emulsifies. Add the cubes of lamb and stir them around to coat them in the marinade. Cover, and put in the refrigerator for at least 6 hours or overnight.

If using wooden skewers, soak them in water for 1 hour before threading the meat and vegetables onto them; if using metal skewers, brush them with oil. Light the barbecue.

Cut the zucchini into quarters lengthwise, and then into 1 1/2-inch/4-cm pieces; cook them in boiling, salted water until just tender. The onions should be cut into 8 pieces, secured with toothpicks/cocktail sticks, and also blanched in boiling, salted water. Cut the bell peppers into bite size pieces.

Thread the meat, onions, zucchini, peppers and tomatoes onto the skewers (remove the toothpicks from the chunks of onion), and brush with a little of the marinade.

Grill on an oiled rack set 5-6 inches/15cm above glowing coals, basting frequently with the marinade and turning occasionally. The lamb will take 15-18 minutes to cook, or less if you like your meat medium rare. Alternatively, put the skewers under a pre-heated broiler/grill; medium well done will take 12 - 15 minutes.

Discard the marinade when you have finished basting - it should not be served with the *shashlik*. Makes 16 skewers.

◆ *Romanian Jews like their kebabs large and liberally flavored with garlic.*

LEG OF LAMB MARINATED IN HERBS

MARINADE
1/2 cup/100ml white wine vinegar
1 cup/225ml olive oil
2 tablespoons fresh thyme,
2 tablespoons fresh rosemary, or
2 teaspoons dried
1 tablespoon fresh oregano, or 1 teaspoon dried
3 tablespoons fresh mint, or 1 tablespoon dried
2 large cloves garlic
1 teaspoon freshly ground black pepper

leg of lamb weighing 3 - 4 lbs/ 1.5-2 kg
12 cloves garlic, halved

Using a food processor, blend together all the marinade ingredients. Place the lamb in a large dish and pour the marinade over it; using a small knife, stab the leg randomly, and insert half a clove of garlic with each stab. Cover and refrigerate for 24 hours, turning occasionally so that the meat thoroughly absorbs the marinade flavors.

Remove from the refrigerator and allow to stand for 1 hour. Transfer the meat to the rack of a broiling pan/grill pan and sprinkle with salt. Pre-heat the broiler/grill and cook for 14 minutes on each side if you like your meat medium well. Alternatively, cook the meat on a rack set 6 inches/20 cm above glowing coals, allowing 12 minutes each side for medium rare.

Transfer the meat to a carving board and allow to stand for 10 minutes before carving. Holding the carving knife at an angle of 45°, slice the lamb thinly across the grain. Serve immediately with grilled vegetables.
Serves 8 to 10.

GRILLED LAMB CHOPS

1/4 teaspoon each of ground allspice,
black pepper, cardamom,
cinnamon and salt
8 lamb chops

Mix the spices and seasonings together and sprinkle over the chops. Put the chops on the barbecue or under a pre-heated broiler/grill and cook on both sides until brown and sizzling. Serve with rice.

◆ *Rosemary*

growing wild

in the grounds

of a monastery

near

Jerusalem.

RED CHICKEN À LA TOURAN

Many chefs and restaurateurs come from
this little village in the Upper Galilee

4 poussins/spring chickens, weighing
1 lb/450g each
3 tablespoons coarse salt
3 onions, sliced
3 cloves garlic, crushed
1/2 teaspoon black pepper
1/2 teaspoon saffron
1/4 teaspoon ground cardamom
1/4 teaspooon ground cloves
2 tablespoons somek *
1/2 cup/100ml olive oil
4 large pitas

Clean the chickens, rub them with salt
inside and out, and refrigerate for 1 hour.
Put the onions and garlic into a shallow
casserole dish just big enough to hold all
four chickens. Mix all the spices together.
Take the chickens out of the refrigerator,
wash them, pat them dry and rub them with
the spice mixture inside and out. Put them
on top of the onions in the casserole dish,
breast up. Refrigerate for several hours.

Transfer the contents of the casserole
dish to a large shallow saucepan, add 2
cups/500ml water, bring to a boil, cover
and cook until the birds are very tender.
The water will evaporate, but if this happens too fast, add a little more. Remove
from the heat and add the olive oil. Transfer
to the casserole dish and broil/grill for 8
minutes. Spread the onions on the 4 *pitas*,
put the chickens on top and broil for another 5 minutes.

*Somek is a red, salty powder that gives a
pleasant flavor to almost any savoury dish. It is
an excellent addition to any spice shelf, but it can
be omitted here if difficult to obtain. Its chief
value in this recipe is its color.

SHISH KEBABS

Ground meat on skewers

12 oz/350g veal
1 1/4 lbs/550g lamb
small bunch parsley
1 onion
4 cloves garlic
1/2 teaspoon allspice
1/2 teaspoon cinnamon
salt and pepper to taste

Grind/mince together the meat, parsley,
onions and garlic. Add the spices and mix
well. Take generous spoonfuls of the mixture and shape into thin sausages. Thread
onto flat metal skewers and broil/grill or put
on the barbecue until they sizzle and begin
to brown. Turn and cook the other side.

In Israel, grilled meat is usually served on
a plate by itself, *pita*, bread, *mezze* and Israeli
salad already being on the table. In the
street, grilled meat is put into *pitas* with
salad and *tahini*, or sold wrapped in the kind
of large *pita* shown on p. 148.

◆ *Red*

chicken

served on

pita

bread.

FISH GRILLED OVER CHARCOAL

2 lbs/900g fish (bass, grouper or red snapper),
or one small fish (bream, gray mullet)
per person
chopped parsley and lemon wedges,
to garnish

MARINADE 1
1/3 cup/80ml olive oil
1 tablespoon salt
1 teaspoon ground allspice
2 tablespoons fresh lemon juice

MARINADE 2
1 onion, cut into rings
2 tablespoons lemon juice
3 tablespoons olive oil
1 tablespoon salt
1/2 teaspoon black pepper
1 clove garlic, finely chopped
1 teaspoon ground cumin
4 bay leaves

Clean and wash the fish, and pat them dry. If you are using large fish, cut them into steaks. Mix the marinade of your choice and pour it into a shallow dish. Add the fish, turning them so that the marinade coats them all over. Allow to marinate for 2 hours.

Remove the fish from the marinade and put them on a lightly oiled grill/rack or onto skewers. Cook over charcoal, turning every 2 or 3 minutes and basting regularly with the marinade. Average cooking time is 15 - 20 minutes, depending on the size of the fish. The skin should be crisp and the flesh flake easily.

Transfer to a serving platter, garnish with parsley and lemon wedges and serve immediately.

SMOKE-GRILLED GROUPER

1 medium grouper
(or sea bass, red snapper, barracuda or bonito)

If you have the luck to meet and catch a grouper on a scuba fishing day, you can have yourself a real feast, and save yourself the hassle of getting the fish home and putting it into an already full refrigerator. You cook it right there on the beach.

Collect three big stones and arrange them in a triangle, with their tops level. Collect dry wood, put it between the stones and make a fire. Clean and scale the fish, rinsing it in sea water. Collect three sticks (or better still find three metal rods), wet them thoroughly, and place them on the stones so that they form a small triangle - this is your grill rack. When the fire starts to die down, place the fish on the rack. Cook for 20 minutes on each side - a fish weighing 4 lbs/2kg takes at least 45 minutes to cook. Now gather fresh herbs such as thyme, rosemary and marjoram (if you are not in Israel you may have to bring them with you!) and smother the fire with them. The aim is to work up a good smoke. Let the fish cure for 1 hour, and be ready to extinguish the herbs with sea water if they catch fire. Eat hot or cold.

 A large grouper absorbing the flavor of fresh herbs over an open fire.

WINE & SPIRITS

◆ *Without quality grapes there can be no quality wines. Wine is now more widely appreciated in Israel.*

Israelis are not drinkers. They may order a bottle of white wine with a meal, or nurse a bottle of beer for a whole evening, or even sit around a table covered with empty bottles, but they are not serious drinkers.

There are many reasons why Israel has never made it into the league table of drinking nations. History for one. Drinking was never a favorite pastime with Jews. They may have sneaked a schnapps in the long, cold winters of Russia or Poland, but most of their social drinking was done on Friday nights and on holidays. Their wine was blessed, but it was sacrificial and sweet, not the kind of wine that goes with dinner. Security is another reason. Despite the unaccountable state of readiness of the armies of various nations of heavy drinkers, we prefer to stay sober. Our unique security problems call for so-briety at all times. Weather is another reason. We have long, hot summers when it is just too hot to drink. When we do, we find that a cold beer, *arak* (an anise-based beverage not unlike ouzo or Pernod), or chilled white wine goes down best. Heavy, syrupy liquers are out and so are whiskies and cognacs.

◆ The trademark of Israel's largest wine maker shows the two biblical spies sent out by Joshua. They returned carrying grapes as proof that the land ahead was "flowing with milk and honey."

The truth is that for many years we had no local wine industry to speak of. Even in ancient times, we were not great wine-makers. Wine culture and wine appreciation in Israel is really a phenomenon of the 1980s.

Most Israeli wineries date from the beginnning of this century. The two largest, in Rishon Lezion and Zichron Yaakov, were founded with the financial support and know-how of Baron de Rothschild. French wine-makers and local farmers planted vines. Two well-equipped wineries were built. But the wine they produced was too sweet to be true table wine. Yet when table wines were finally produced, the makers discovered that it was almost impossible to market them in Israel. The gourmet revolution that hit us in the eighties had not yet arrived. So although we had drinkable wine, we had no food to drink it with. In those days we had Sauvignon Blanc and Cabernet Sauvignon, and the

◆ Israel's first winery was founded by Baron de Rothschild in Rishon Lezion.

occasional bottle of Semillion or Colombard. These were distributed to small neighborhood stores where they were propped upright in direct sunlight. Of course they spoiled quickly. When the tentative gourmet tried his first bottle, it was sour, which naturally discouraged him.

So for the time being we stuck to beer. Our founding fathers realised that beer was the most fitting alcoholic beverage for a hot and busy country. Beer is a thirst quencher. It is filling, the liquid equivalent of bread. It is also a natural foil to the hot, peppery foods we are so fond of. We have three local brands of beer, more or less. All of them are adequate, but one of them - a clear and flavorsome European-style pilsner - is superb.

When the great food revolution finally came, Israel's wine producers were quick off the mark. To see how this happened, we must go back a decade or so. The first decent Israeli wine was fermented and bottled on the Golan Heights at the Golan Winery. Wine-growing on the Golan was the bright idea of a moshavnik who was very successful with apples. The soil of the Golan is unique, the result of volcanic eruptions that once shook the whole region. The cool upland climate - cold at night, pleasantly warm during the day, liberally sprinkled with rain, seldom touched by frosts - is also ideal for grape-growing.

In the early 1980s, after a few years of trial runs under the supervision of an American wine-maker from California, Golan produced its first commercial vintage, a very dry and distinctive Sauvignon Blanc. In the

◆ *The original site of the first winery in Rishon Lezion.*

◆ *The winemaster at work.*

◆ *A container of grapes harvested in the early morning is quickly sent to the winery.*

belief that it would be much easier to win honors abroad than sell their carefully perfected product at home, Golan sought and found an appreciative market in Europe and the United States. Their wine was a great success abroad. Not only was it good, it was also from Israel, where wine had been produced for centuries!

With chestfuls of medals and citations from international wine shows, Golan started to tackle the home market. Their timing was perfect. While their wines had been conquering the world, Israel had undergone its long-awaited gastronomic revolution. I do not use the word revolution lightly. The change was dramatic. Hundred of restaurants opened almost overnight, and the emphasis shifted away from Middle Eastern and Arab cuisine to International. For the first time we had an opportunity to find out what we really liked - French, Japanese, Italian, American....Acquiring a taste for good wine was a natural progression. When that happened, Golan was ready with new and exciting wines.

Today, instead of three home-grown wines to choose from, we have twenty-five. The old sweet wines were no longer commercially viable, and with Golan setting the pace, other wineries had no choice but to join the race. Wine began to be promoted and discussed. Wine societies and wine newsletters appeared. There were aggressive advertising campaigns, with each winery claiming supremacy. Consumers were faced with an array of labels and styles of wine. Prices were high to begin with, but increasing demand has brought them down.

We are still not a nation of wine-drinkers as the French or Italians are, but if we do decide to celebrate, we have good local wine to celebrate with.

WINE & SPIRITS

Recipes

GROUPER WITH FENNEL & ARAK

*1 large grouper (or sea bass, or red snapper),
scaled and cleaned
(allow 12 oz/350g per person)
4 bulbs fennel, thinly sliced
salt and freshly ground white pepper
2 onions, thinly sliced
3 cloves garlic, crushed
1/2 cup/100ml olive oil
1/2 cup/100ml arak (or ouzo, or any other
anise-flavored liqueur)*

Season the inside of the fish and the slices of fennel with salt and pepper. Mix the onions, garlic and olive oil with the fennel, and stuff the fish with half of this mixture. Cover the bottom of an earthenware baking dish with the rest, place the fish on top, cover the dish with foil, and bake in a moderate oven (350°F/180°C). A large fish will take about 1 hour to cook, a smaller one less than half that time. Warm the *arak*, pour it over the fish as it comes out of the oven, and set light to it. Serve as soon as the flames have died down.

 Grouper

with fennel

and arak.

BREAST OF MOULLARD IN WINE SAUCE

The moullard is a cross between a goose and a Berber duck.

*2 moullard breasts (or duck, or goose),
weighing 12 oz/350g each
1 onion, finely diced
2 tablespoons dried cherries
1/4 teaspoon black pepper
pinch brown sugar
1 cup/225ml dry red wine
3 tablespoons rich brown sauce base/stock
4 tablespoons butter*

Prick the breasts a few times with a fork, then lay them in a cold, heavy skillet/frying pan, fatty side down. Cook over a medium heat until the breasts color a deep brown, then add the onion, cherries, pepper and sugar. Turn the breasts, and add the wine and sauce base/stock. Remove the breasts, slice them, and transfer them to a warm serving dish. Reduce the contents of the skillet to a quarter, then remove from the heat and stir in the butter. Spoon over the slices of breast and serve straight away, with roast potatoes. Moullard should never be over-cooked. Serves 4.

◆ *Breast of*

moullard in

wine sauce.

GOOSE LIVER FLAMBÉ

*4 oz/100g goose liver per person, well chilled
salt, white pepper
freshly grated orange rind
Halleluya liqueur (orange-based) or
Grand Marnier
rich brown sauce base/stock*

Carefully cut the liver into slices 1/3 inch/0.8cm thick. Season with salt and pepper, and chill in the refrigerator.

Heat a heavy skillet/frying pan and sauté the slices for about 2 seconds on each side - no oil is needed since goose liver contains a lot of fat. Pour off excess fat for future use. Add a sprinkling of orange rind, 1 tablespoon of brown sauce base and 2 tablespoons of heated liqueur. Set alight with a match and serve immediately. This superb delicacy should be served by itself, accompanied by nothing but a good white wine.

SAUCE BASE

Most classic cookbooks contain a recipe for a rich brown sauce base made from beef, beef bones and vegetables. In Israel we make something very similar, often cooking it overnight and serving it as a soup.

◆ *Goose liver*

flambeéd

in orange

liqueur.

STUFFED PIGEONS

1 cup/225g rice
6 pigeons, plucked and cleaned, with livers
5 cloves garlic, crushed
1 cup/150g chopped walnuts or pistachios
4 tablespoons chopped parsley
salt and freshly ground black pepper
pinch ground cardamom
freshly grated nutmeg, to taste
vegetable oil
3 onions, sliced
1 carrot, sliced
1 teaspoon celery salt
4 cups/1 liter black non-alcoholic malt beer
1/2 cup/100ml brandy

Boil the rice in salted water for 12 minutes, then drain well. Cut the pigeon livers into cubes, then mix with the rice, 3 of the garlic cloves, the nuts, parsley and spices. Stuff the birds loosely with this mixture and close the openings with skewers. Fry the birds for 5 minutes on each side (a Dutch oven would give better results in this recipe), put them on their backs, then add the rest of the garlic, the onion, carrot and celery salt to the pan. Sauté for 10 minutes, then add the malt beer and brandy and transfer to an ovenproof dish.

Cover and bake for 2 hours in an oven pre-heated to 300°F/150°C. When the birds are cooked, the flesh should come easily off the bones. Uncover and continue cooking for another 15 minutes. Add a little more malt beer if the birds look dry. Put the birds on individual plates to serve. Strain the sauce, spoon a little over the birds and serve the rest in a jug. Serves 4 to 6, accompanied by pickles.

COMPOTE OF DRIED FRUIT IN RED WINE

equal quantities of dried apricots prunes, raisins, dates and blanched almonds
2 cloves
2 cardamom pods
1 stick cinnamon
red wine
whipped cream, to serve

Soak the fruit in cold water for 10 minutes, then discard the water. Put all the fruit, the almonds and the spices in a heavy saucepan, and add enough red wine to cover them. Bring to a boil, then simmer for 12 minutes, stirring occasionally. Take out the cloves, cardamom and cinnamon, and allow to cool. Cover and refrigerate. Serve in individual glasses with whipped cream in a separate bowl.

ROSEHIP COCKTAIL

1 lb/450g rosehips, preferably from damask roses
1 cup/225g sugar
1/2 cup/100ml lemon juice
2 cups/500ml rosé wine
1 cup/225ml white rum
juice of 1 pomegranate, optional

Wash the rosehips, cover in water and refrigerate for 4 hours. Boil the rosehips until they are soft, then strain the liquid into another saucepan and discard the rosehips. Add the sugar and boil for 5 minutes, then add the rest of the ingredients and chill. Serve with ice, with rose petals for decoration.

◆ *Stuffed pigeon with baby eggplants.*

◆ *Compote of dried fruit in red wine.*

FRUITS &
DESSERTS

◆ *A feast of*

ripe figs

and peeled

prickly

pears.

The Hebrew word *sabra* means prickly, thorny, rough. A *sabra* (plural *sabres*) is a prickly pear, a regional and popular fruit, but it also describes an Israeli stereotype, an Israeli-born Israeli complete with all the traits typical of his or her fruity namesake. The epithet has been in use for so many years now that we have stopped being offended by it, and at times we even take a certain pride in it. How many other nations are named after a fruit?

For a time the name was appropriate. Prickly pears are thorny. They have a thick skin. They have a short season - less than two months in summer. They are extremely difficult to pick and they used not to be sold commercially, or at least not on a large scale. But when you do pick them, and remove the thorns, and peel them, and cut them open, they are sweet and unique in taste and texture. If a whole nation must be named after a fruit, perhaps *sabra* is not such a bad name.

◆ *When you buy a watermelon the greengrocer willingly cuts out a little piece for you to try.*

We used to buy prickly pears from the back of very small carts, most of them pushed along by kids who would clean the fruit and hand it to you on the street. You ate it straight away. It was rather special, something you could not buy by the kilo like other fruit. Then the plant breeders stepped in.

The prickly pear is now in decline, a victim of commercial sophistication. A new, improved,

◆ *Watermelon*

stands appear

in summer

and vanish

when the

season is over.

thornless, perennial *sabra* is now available. The moral of this story is that the *sabra* may no longer stand for what we are, unless of course we too have become new, improved, thornless and perennial.

The abundance of fruit in Israel is staggering. The fruit we grow today knows no season. Grapes start in spring and continue through to November. Watermelons and melons start in March and go on through September. Citrus fruit is available all year round. It is an amazing sight. The typical Israeli fruit stall is lush and heavy with fruit in all seasons, all ripe, all sweet, all ready to eat. And as if indigenous species were not enough, in the last few years we have also managed to grow tropical and exotic fruit - papaya/pawpaw and kiwi fruit, Sharon fruit/persimmons and carambolas, passionfruit and pineapples, lychees and kumquats, dates and figs, Chinese apples and feijoas. Every season brings a new arrival.

It has become almost a tradition that every year some far-seeing and resourceful moshav or kibbutz will introduce a new fruit that it has secretly nursed to perfection, forcing it to adapt to local conditions. Young botonists are busy changing the size and color of watermelons - they want the new generation of watermelons to be smaller, sweeter and seedless. They are also changing the shape and size of pickling vegetables. It is easier, they say, to pickle round cucumbers than long ones, so they are growing cucumbers that look like green tomatoes. Some of these exciting fruits survive for one season and never return. If they do not prove commercially attractive, why grow them? But there is alway as another designer fruit in the wings.

We put our great variety of fruit to good use. For example, it almost compulsory for all house-

◆ Rahat lokum, *Turkish delight, is still made by hand in an old factory in Jerusalem.*

◆ *Assorted candies by Havillo of Jerusalem.*

◆ *Fruit boulevard in affluent Ramat Hasharon, a suburb of Tel Aviv. The simultaneous display of summer and winter fruit is an Israeli phenomenon.*

◆ *Fruit*

boulevard in

affluent

Ramat Hasharon,

a suburb of

Tel Aviv.

The simultaneous

display of

summer and

winter fruit is

an Israeli

phenomenon.

holds to offer a large selection of fresh fruit, dried fruit and nuts to inmates and visitors. Fruit is not something we buy for special occasions. It is a staple. We eat it all the time. In fact it is a wonder that such a fruity nation ever bothers with cakes and pastries. Yet cakes and sweet desserts are an integral part of the culinary cultures of all the ethnic minorities living in Israel, and none of them has yet given up cakes in favor of fruit.

Baklava and *konafa* are the grandest of Arab pastries, although their origin is probably Turkish or Greek. They are made at home and commercially. Proud housewives may scorn store-bought pastries, but most are fresh and tasty and a good bet for those who do not want to bother. *Baklava* and *konafa* should be light, crisp and delicate, and the fillings should consist of pistachios and walnuts, and not peanuts. Although they look elaborate, *baklava* and *konafa* are easy to prepare, and they are dual-purpose, desserts as well pastries to be consumed with coffee or tea. No party or grand occasion is complete without them.

Another essential of Israeli dessert is Turkish coffee. A lot of myth and folklore is attached to the small demi-tasse cups of strong, fragrant liquid. The Bedouins brew their coffee in narrow-necked, long-handled pots called *finjans* or *tanakas*, which come in various sizes. Their coffee is made from very finely ground coffee beans to which a few cardamom seeds have been added, and it is drunk  thick, strong, and usually very sweet. The coffee is boiled in the *finjan* seven times before it is served, the repeated boilings producing a froth which is very tasty and part of the enjoyment.

$\mathscr{F}$ RUITS & DESSERTS

◆ *Old and new.*
Jaffa oranges
have a world-
wide reputation,
but Israeli
strawberries are
less well known.
Every year
they get bigger
and better.

$\mathscr{R}ecipes$

BAKLAVA
Layered pastry with nuts and syrup

1 lb/450g filo pastry (about 24 sheets)
1 cup/225g unsalted butter, melted
10 oz/275g pistachio nuts, walnuts or almonds,
coarsely chopped
2 tablespoons sugar

SYRUP
1 heaped cup/250g sugar
1/2 cup/100ml water
1 tablespoon lemon juice
1 tablespoon orange blossom water

To make the syrup, dissolve the sugar in the water and lemon juice, and simmer until it is thick enough to coat the back of a spoon. Add the orange blossom water and simmer for another 2 minutes. Allow to cool, then chill in the refrigerator.

To cook the *filo* pastry you will need a large round or square baking pan. Brush the bottom and sides of the pan with the melted butter, then lay half the *filo* sheets in the pan, brushing each sheet with melted butter as you lay it in and overlapping the sheets or folding the sides over as necessary. Pre-heat the oven to 350°-375°F/180°-190°C. Mix the chopped nuts with the sugar and sprinkle evenly over the top sheet of *filo*. Now lay the rest of the sheets of *filo* in the pan, brushing with butter as before. Brush the top sheet with melted butter. Using a very sharp knife, cut the pastry diagonally into diamond shapes.

Bake for 30 minutes at 350°-375°F/180°-190°C, then raise the oven temperature to 450°-475°F/230°-250°C and cook for another 15 minutes. The *baklava* should be very puffy and light gold in color. Remove from the oven and immediately pour the chilled syrup over the hot pastry. Leave in the dish to cool.

To serve, cut along the diagonal lines and arrange on a serving dish; alternatively, turn out upside down onto a large plate, put another plate on the bottom, turn the right way up, then cut along the original lines.

FROSTED ROSES
A very luxurious and special garnish for desserts

10 unblemished roses, half open,
with their stems
4 egg whites
4 or 5 tablespoons water
2 cups/450g sugar/castor sugar

Choose mostly red roses, and roses which have not been sprayed! Shop-bought roses have been sprayed, so pick roses from your own garden. Rose petals are edible and tasty.

Thoroughly stir (do not whip/whisk) the water into the egg whites and dip the heads of the roses into it, moving them about so that all the petals become coated with the mixture. Now stand the stems in a bowl and leave for 10 minutes. Using a sugar sifter, dust the flowers heavily with sugar. Do the same with any loose petals. Now hang the roses up by their stalks and let them dry for 2 days. Then put them on a tray and let them dry for another 3 days. Store carefully in an airtight container or in the freezer. Use for decorating custards and other desserts. Providing they are well coated with egg white and thoroughly dried, frosted roses should keep for up to 6 months.

◆ *Layered pastries*

with nuts and

syrup come in

different shapes

and flavors.

◆ *Sesame*

and

peanut

bars.

CONFIT OF FIGS

2 lbs/900g whole fresh figs
4 cups/900g sugar
1/2 cup/100 ml water
2oz/60g sesame seeds
2oz/60g blanched almonds
2 tablespoons fresh lemon juice

Wash the figs and prick them a few times with a fork. Dissolve the sugar in the water, add the figs, sesame seeds, almonds and lemon juice, and simmer over a very low heat for 2 hours. At the end of this time the figs should look almost transparent. Cool and serve at room temperature.

SESAME BARS

3oz/75g sesame seeds
1-1/2 cups/350g sugar
3/4 cup/175ml water
1 teaspoon cinnamon
pinch ground cloves
1/2 teaspoon lemon juice

Using a non-stick skillet/frying pan, fry the sesame seeds until they are golden (no fat is required because sesame seeds are rich in oil). Dissolve the sugar in the water, bring to a boil and continue boiling until the sugar begins to turn golden brown. At this point, add the sesame seeds, cinnamon, cloves and lemon juice, and continue to stir for 3 minutes. Remove from the heat, pour onto a wet marble slab and, using a wet rolling pin, roll the mixture to an even thickness of about 1/2 inch/1 cm. Using a fish slice or pallet knife, quickly lever the toffee off the marble slab and cut it into bars. Alternatively, leave it to harden and then snap it into chunks. Keep in an airtight container. Bars of almond or pine nut brittle can be made in the same way.

CANDIED ORANGE & GRAPEFRUIT PEEL

2 large oranges
2 thick-skinned grapefruit
4 1/2 cups/1kg sugar
2 cups/450ml water
juice of 1 lemon

◆ *Candied*

orange

and

grapefruit

peel.

Scrub the skins of the fruit with a hard brush, then cut them in half and scoop out the flesh. Put the half shells into a bowl of water, cover with a plate, and soak for 2 days, changing the water once during this time. Drain and cut into strips. Put the strips into a large saucepan, cover with water, bring to a boil and simmer for 15 minutes. Pour off the water. Cover with water again, bring to a boil, simmer for 15 minutes, and drain. Repeat the process once more.

Now add the sugar and 2 cups of water to the peel, bring to a boil and simmer very gently for 2 hours, with the lid of the saucepan off. When all the liquid has evaporated, stir in the lemon juice, making sure that it coats all the pieces of peel. Drain the peel and cut it into bite-sized pieces. Roll the pieces in sugar if you like but this is not absolutely necessary. Leave on a plate or on wax/greaseproof paper for several hours to harden. Store in an airtight container.

◆ *Confit*

of figs.

TANGERINE SORBET

1 cup/225g sugar
1 cup/225 ml water
2 lbs/900g tangerines
1/2 grapefruit
1 teaspoon Cointreau or orange liqueur

Dissolve the sugar in the water and bring to a boil. Cook for 5 minutes, remove from the heat and allow to cool. Pare the zest from 3 of the tangerines and reserve. Remove the segments from half the tangerines and carefully peel them. Squeeze the juice from the rest of the tangerines and from the grapefruit.

Blend together the syrup, zest, juice and liqueur, pour into a bowl and freeze and whip/whisk. Repeat the whipping every 20 minutes or so, two or three more times, so that the sorbet stays soft when frozen. Serve decorated with the tangerine segments.

BAKED APPLES

10 cooking apples
1 cup/225 ml red wine
2 tablespoons sugar
1 teaspoon powdered cinnamon
1 cup/150g raisins
1/4 cup/60g melted butter
Grand Marnier or orange liqueur, optional

Wash and core the apples, but do not cut right through to the base. Arrange the apples in a greased baking pan and pre-heat the oven to 350°F/180°C.

Mix together the wine, sugar, cinnamon and raisins and spoon a little of the mixture into each apple. Top with melted butter. Bake for about 1 hour. Serve hot or cold, with a teaspoon of Grand Marnier on top, if liked.

BAKED QUINCE OLYMPUS

5 quinces
2 pints/1 liter water
1 1/2 lbs/700g sugar
1 1/4 cups/300ml lemon juice
3 whole sticks cinnamon

Trim the quinces at both ends and cut them in half lengthwise. Peel them, then soak them in water with a little lemon juice added to it to prevent them from discoloring.

Dissolve two-thirds of the sugar in the water and bring to a boil. Add the lemon juice, cinnamon and quince halves and simmer for 15-25 minutes, or until the quinces are soft (prick them with a fork to see if they are tender). Place the quinces in a baking pan, cut side up, pour the syrup over them and sprinkle with the rest of the sugar. Bake in an oven pre-heated to 450°F/230°C until they are a dark golden color. Turn off the oven. Leave the quinces in the oven to cool. Serve at room temperature.

Serves 10.

◆ *Baked quince.*

◆ *Baked apple stuffed with raisins.*

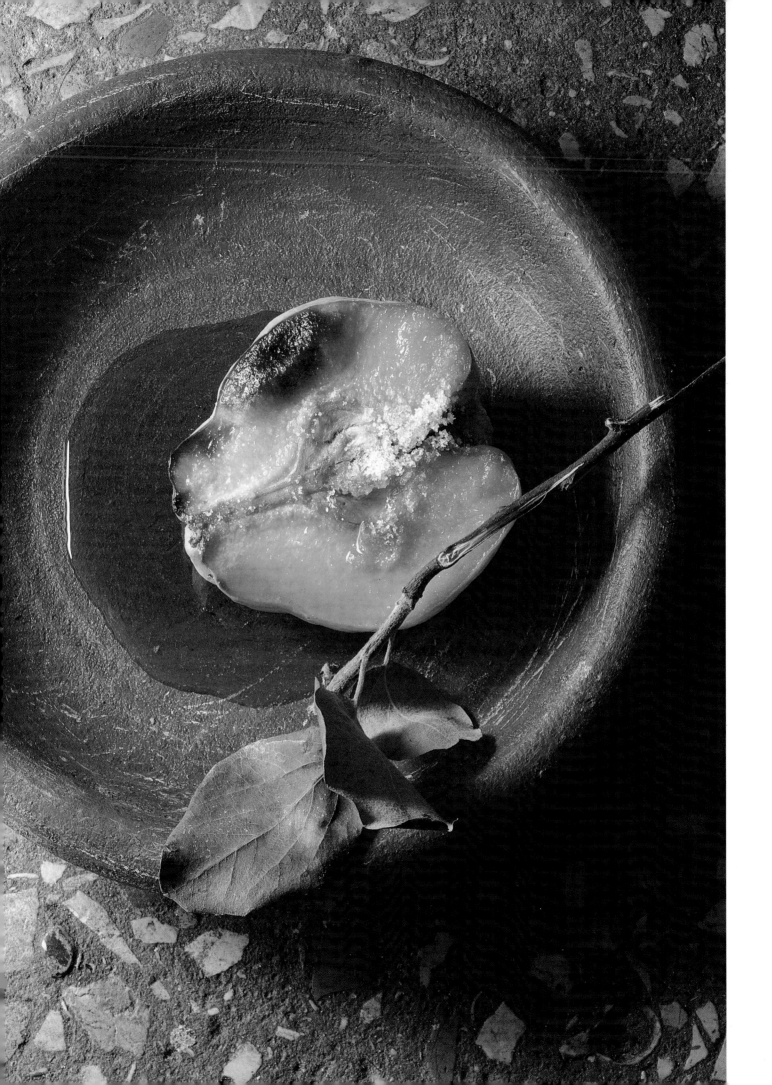

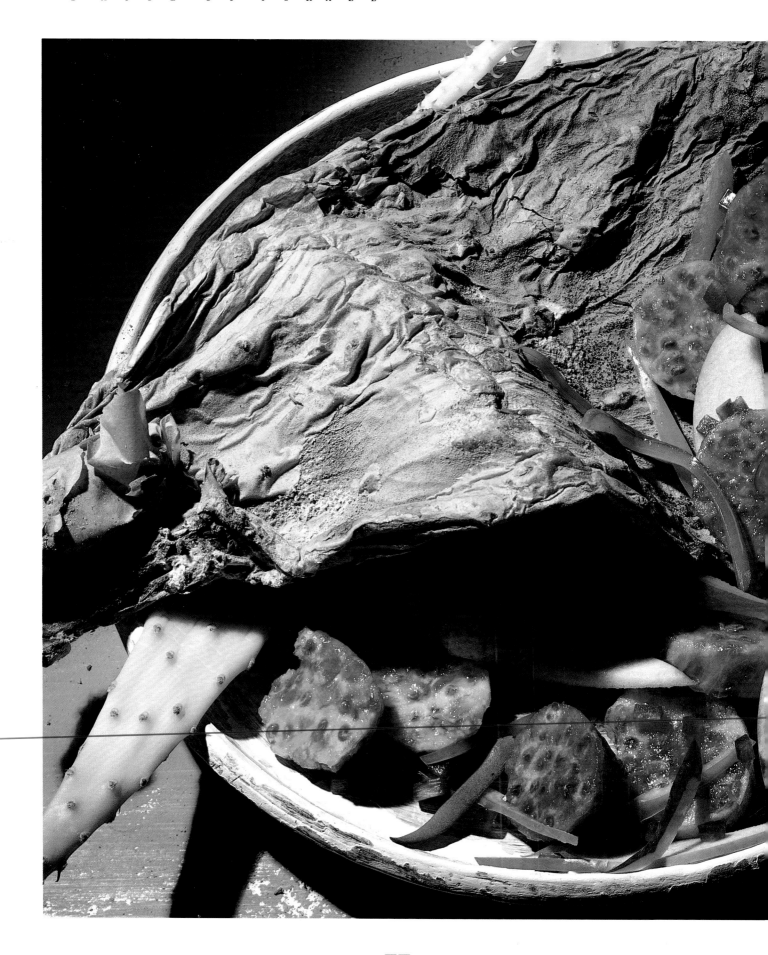

◆ *Prickly*

pear

salad.

PRICKLY PEAR SALAD

juice of 1 orange
juice of 1 lemon
1/2 teaspoon powdered cardamom
1 tablespoon nut oil
3 prickly pears
2 dessert apples, cut into small strips
1 red bell pepper, cut into small strips
pinch hot chili pepper

Combine the orange juice, lemon juice, cardamom and nut oil in a salad bowl. Carefully peel the prickly pears under running water, making shallow incisions in the flesh to remove the roots of the thorns. Slice and add to the bowl, together with the strips of apple, red pepper and cucumber. Sprinkle with a little chili powder, toss well and serve with other salads at the dinner table.

PRICKLY PEAR SAUCE

8 prickly pears
juice of 1/2 lemon
2 1/2 tablespoons Kirsch
2 level teaspoons arrowroot

Carefully peel the prickly pears. Chop them, then rub the flesh through a nylon sieve into a small saucepan. Add the lemon juice and Kirsch and warm through. Mix the arrowroot to a smooth paste with a little cold water, then stir it into the purée and Kirsch mixture. Bring to a boil and simmer gently for 2 or 3 minutes until the mixture turns syrupy. Serve hot or cold with fruit sorbets or brochettes of grilled fruit.

MA'AMOUL
Small pastries filled with dates & nuts

FILLING
4 oz/100g dried dates, pitted
4 oz/100g walnuts, coarsely chopped
4 oz/100g almonds or pistachio nuts, coarsely chopped
2/3 cup/150ml water
4 oz/100g sugar
1 heaped teaspoon ground cinnamon

DOUGH
4 cups/450g all-purpose/plain flour
1 cup/225g unsalted butter, melted
2 tablespoons rosewater
4 or 5 tablespoons milk
confectioner's/icing sugar

To prepare the filling, chop the dates, put them into a saucepan with the chopped nuts, water, sugar and cinnamon, and cook over a low heat until the dates are soft and the water has been absorbed.

To make the dough, sift the flour into a bowl, add the melted butter and lightly cut/rub it in. Add the rosewater and milk, and knead to a softish consistency. Divide the dough into walnut size pieces. Pre-heat the oven to 300°F/150°C.

Taking a piece of dough at a time, roll it into a ball between your palms, then hollow it out with your thumb, pinching the sides up to make a large thimble shape. Now fill the thimble with a little of the date mixture and press the dough back over the filling to make a ball. Slightly flatten the ball in the palm of your hand and use a fork to make an interesting pattern on top · straight lines are the traditional pattern.

When you have used up all the dough and filling, place the *ma'moul* on a greased baking sheet and bake for about 30 minutes. Do not allow them to brown or they will become hard. When they are cold, roll them in confectioner's sugar and store in an airtight tin.

HALVAH SOUFFLÉ

6 sponge fingers
6oz/175g halvah
2 level tablespoons/30g cornstarch/cornflour
2 tablespoons sugar
pinch salt
6 egg yolks and 4 egg whites
2 tablespoons brandy
1 cup/225 ml milk
2 level tablespoons/30g all-purpose/plain flour

For this you will need a 2 pint/l liter soufflé dish. Butter and flour the inside, and shake out any excess flour. Line the bottom with sponge fingers, trimming them to fit.

Crumble the halvah and mix to a smooth paste with a little water. Add the cornstarch, half the sugar, a pinch of salt, the 6 egg yolks and the brandy, and mix thoroughly. Heat the milk almost to boiling point, then pour it into the halvah mixture, beating non-stop with a fork as you do so. Now sift in the flour, give the mixture a brisk whip/whisk, and leave to cool. Pre-heat the oven to 400°F/210°C.

Whip/whisk the egg whites to stiff peaks with the rest of the sugar. Stir one third into the halvah mixture, and carefully fold in the rest. Pour into the prepared soufflé dish, put into the oven and bake for 25 minutes. Do not open the oven door while the soufflé is in – if there is a chance of the top burning, place a sheet of greased foil on top as you put the soufflé into the oven.

Serve immediately.

◆ Ma'amoul

are small

pastries

filled with

dates and

nuts

◆ Halvah

and thick

Turkish

coffee with

cardamom.

BISKOTCHOS

Crisp, salty tea-time cookies shaped like
bagels

1oz/25g yeast
1/2 teaspoon sugar
1 cup/225g lukewarm water
3 cups/350g all purpose/plain flour, sifted
*3/4 cup/200g margarine or shortening/lard, in
small pieces*
1 level teaspoon salt
1 tablespoon oil
*powdered anise, cumin or coriander, optional
sesame seeds*

Dissolve the yeast and the sugar in a little of
the water and leave for 10 minutes. Make a
well in the flour and add the margarine or
shortening, the salt, the oil, the yeast mixture and the rest of the water. Add a little
anise, cumin or coriander too, if liked. Knead
to a smooth elastic dough. Cover and leave
in a warm place for 1 hour. Pre-heat the
oven to 350°F/190°C.

Divide the dough into 25-30 walnut-sized
pieces. Sprinkle a board with sesame seeds
and roll each piece into a
pencil shape about 4
inches/10cm long, mak-
ing sure it is well coated
with sesame seeds. Pinch
the ends together to form
small rings. Arrange on
an oiled baking sheet and
bake for 45 minutes. Store
in an airtight container.

◆ *A Jericho*

fruit and

vegetable

vendor takes

an afternoon

tea break.

◆ *Mint*

tea and

biskotchos.

NEW ISRAELI CHEFS

Some of my best friends are cooks, and they are a strange lot. They stay up far into the night trying to remember the exact two weeks in spring when white Judean truffles bloom. If cornered, they will admit that the white Judean truffle, collected by Bedouins in the Judean desert, is not worth losing sleep over. It is a dry, powdery object, but it's the only truffle we've got, and we have to be patriotic. If we were not patriots, why on earth would we live in a country that does not have truffles, oysters, clams, lobsters and decent shrimps, which the laws of *kashrut* forbid us to cook in any case.

My friends also sit by their windows at night waiting for rain, for when it rains the fish are fresh and firm and the mushrooms grow. When I point out that the only mushroom that grows here is gooey and fleshy and requires

hours of cleaning, which spoils both the taste and the texture, they get furious.

Our gallant new chefs are first in the produce markets, poking the tomatoes, squeezing the lettuces, listening to the watermelons and angrily turning down fish with dull eyes. The merchants spot them a mile off. For you, they say, we have a catch of red mullet, just off the boat. See how bright and red their skin is. Come on, insist my friends, show us the good stuff. And the good stuff is always there, hidden at the back of large refrigerators, well away from Philistines. They squeeze the fish and purse their lips. It is not in the prime of youth and vigor, but it will have to do. Trout is delivered from the north once a week, and if they do not buy now they will be troutless for a whole week. It does not do to disappoint one's customers too often.

These, then, are the new Israeli chefs, although they have no use for the word "chef". They are cooks. They love good food. They adore new ideas. They attempt the impossible. They have a mission: to create an Israeli cuisine. There are food critics who believe it is a suicide mission. There are no more culinary frontiers, they say, no more gastronomic wildernesses to be discovered or created. Everyone has been everywhere and eaten everything. Israeli food is what it is and will always be, a lively hybrid, a medley of hits - a little Arab spice, a touch of the Orient, a dash of Eastern Europe, and the zest of fresh produce locally grown.

My friends beg to differ. Every once in a while they sit down and write new recipes, describing at length the new factor in the formula. For example, if you take avocados and make a soup out of them, omitting coriander and adding hyssop, the result is no longer Mexican but Israeli. Hyssop, an in-

digenous and biblical herb, has wrought a species change. If you leave out the pigeon in stuffed pigeon and use quail instead, the result is not French but Israeli. Our forefathers ate quail in the desert. Quail are our heritage. In fact it took us a long time to raise quail in captivity, but we managed it, so we must make the most of them. There is more. If you fry goat's cheese in batter and add mango sauce, and if both the cheese and the mangoes are locally produced, the result is 101 per cent Israeli. It cannot be anything else.

Israel's new cooks fortify themselves behind hot stoves, write books, and appear on television, but it is still too early to claim total victory over the critics. Their quest for a specifically Israeli culinary identity is sometimes spurious. Ever since Jordan severed its ties with the West Bank, Arab olive oil producers have been burdened with a glut of oil, of which only a portion can be consumed by Israelis, so now is not the time to be claiming olive oil as an Israeli invention. They also call Israeli an amazing carrot which grows only in Gaza; it is a vivid purple, crisp, tasty, and marvellous for garnishing. Their quest is also frustrated by the here-today, gone-tomorrow phenomenon. This was exactly the case with fresh ginger.

Ginger is widely used in Chinese and Japanese cooking of course, and was introduced here a few years ago. A few farmers began to grow it and there was a big publicity campaign, heartily endorsed by an Israeli cook who is an expert on Chinese cooking. Everywhere you went, people talked about ginger. A year later, the ginger was gone. The cook who had promoted it so hard called his supplier. Where is my ginger? he asked. Not profitable enough, replied the farmer. It never really caught on. What do you mean profitable? shouted the cook. Everyone's been talking about it. People bought bushels of the stuff. No, said the farmer, it was left to rot in the market. No one bought it.

And that was the end of the Israeli ginger dream. The Chinese-style cook still uses it, but he relies on friends and customers to bring it back from abroad.

Then there was the saga of the quail eggs. Where there is a female quail, there are eggs, and these eggs are ideal for pickling and cooking. Test kitchens around the country worked hard to come up with an original recipe. They were very close, so close they could almost taste it, but the closer they got the scarcer the tiny eggs became. What has happened to our eggs? they asked, and the hardy moshavnik who had promised them a lifetime's supply mumbled something about the productivity of quails going down in captivity. In captivity, it seemed, the quails were too crowded and too scared to lay eggs. We'll pay for larger cages, said the experimental cooks. We must have the eggs. Forget about the eggs, said the moshavnik. I have a new product: eels. How do you feel about eels?

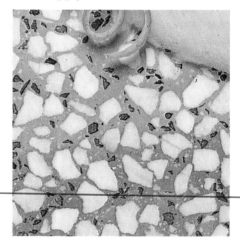

There was indeed something fishy about the farmer's story. Eventually the eggless cooks found out that quail eggs have strange healing properties, including the ability to cure asthma and allergies. The farmer who produced them had opened several fresh quail egg snack bars and was doing terrific business. People were driving in, quaffing the fresh eggs, and driving out feeling a lot better. No shipping, no packing, no mess.

A farmer from the southern part of Israel showed up recently with a sample of Japanese *shitake* mushrooms. He was sent packing.

New chefs also have to contend with a body of opinion which thinks it improper to promote good food and wine. These Jeremiahs see food as part of a long tradition of atonement and suffering. They like to believe that austerity is still with us, that none of our political problems have been solved, that we perch permanently on the brink of war, that the economy is on the skids. They eat to survive, not to celebrate life. To discuss the merits of beluga caviar or the bouquet of a new wine is decadent and irresponsible. There is nothing admirable or artistic about the preparation of food. They care about Israel, not about what Israelis eat.

Perhaps to escape the debilitating effects of such rhetoric our new cooks travel a lot. They must keep up. They go to food conventions, attend demonstrations and give lectures. Their peers judge them less harshly than their compatriots. They always have the avocado to fall back on, and the whole range of citrus fruits. They win medals, which give them great comfort, but they do not wear them at home. They make contacts, and if they are lucky they get invited to the great kitchens of Europe. Roger Verge might ask them to drop by and spend a few days nosing around the kitchen. Anton Mosimann at the Dorchester in London is known to be co-operative; he is a great host, free with advice, outgoing and friendly. Once a year they feel honor-bound to make it to Paris.

This is an expensive but priceless exercise, during which they visit lots of two-star restaurants and lay bets as to which will receive the coveted third star in the next Michelin. They go to Fouchon and spend silly amounts of money on canned truffles (of the Périgord variety), herb vinegars and extra-virgin olive oil. If the oysters at the fish market are fresh, they buy a cooler, fill it with crushed ice and cram it with a few dozen oysters. You can always recognize a new chef on the plane home. He's the one who sits upright for five hours clutching a giant ice box to his chest.

He and his peers belong to a culinary grapevine. He will be the first to know if an Iranian refugee escapes the ayatollahs with a cart of caviar. He is also a guru. Sheep farmers will carry whole sides of lamb up six flights of stairs to get his honest opinion. Deep-sea fishermen will seek him out if a stray lobster gets entangled in their nets.

What has emerged from all this is a young, bold and innovative cuisine. It has been worth waiting for. Cooking is one of those rare professions where the process is as rewarding as the end result.

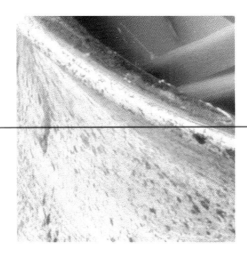

NEW ISRAELI CHEFS

Recipes

HAIM COHEN

◆ *Haim Cohen,*

is the young

chef of Keren

à la Carte,

a French

restaurant.

Cohen

frequently

visits France

to study under

a master chef.

LAMB CUTLETS WITH BAKED TOMATOES

MARINADE
1 cup/225ml dry red wine
1/4 cup/60ml olive oil
3 cloves garlic, unpeeled and crushed
1 bay leaf
fresh thyme and rosemary
1 onion, sliced
1 carrot, sliced
salt and freshly ground black pepper

rack of lamb containing 12 cutlets
4 or 5 large tomatoes

Mix together the marinade ingredients and marinate the lamb for 24 hours. Remove the lamb from the marinade, and trim the flesh and fat from the ends of the bones so that the cutlets are easy to pick up. Pre-heat the oven to 425°F/220°C.

Drain the lamb and thoroughly rub the strained marinade liquor into it before placing in a baking tray and roasting in the oven for 10 minutes. Turn down the heat to 350°F/180°C and cook for another 15 minutes, basting with the cooking juices.

Remove the rack of lamb from the oven, and allow it to rest for 5 minutes before separating the cutlets. Meanwhile add some of the marinade to the cooking juices and reduce over a high heat. Spoon this over the cutlets as you serve them.

The tomatoes, sliced in half, sprinkled with sea salt and fresh thyme and placed on an oiled baking tray, can be baked with the lamb; in a moderate oven, they take about 15 minutes. Serves 4 or 5.

MINTED MELON WITH DATES AND ARAK

16 dried dates, pitted and finely chopped
12 leaves fresh mint, finely chopped
1/2 cup/100ml arak *(or ouzo)*
3 small melons

Marinate the chopped dates and mint in the *arak* for 3 hours. Cut the melons in half, remove the seeds, and fill with the date and mint mixture. Chill before serving.
Serves 6.

SALAD ROCKET WITH PINE NUTS

2 lbs/900g salad rocket
16 spinach leaves
1 romaine/cos lettuce
3 tomatoes
olive oil
salt and pepper
3/4 cup/175g toasted pine nuts

Wash and pat dry all the greens, and remove the stems of the rocket. Cut the tomatoes into thin slices and shred the lettuce.

Spread the rocket and pine nuts on a bed of lettuce and arrange a circle of tomato slices on top. Add another layer of rocket and pine nuts and a layer of spinach, and season with the olive oil, salt and pepper. Serves 6 to 8.

◆ *Lamb cutlets*

with baked

tomatoes.

AVOCADO SOUP

1/2 onion, finely chopped
1/4 cup/60g margarine
3 tablespoons all-purpose/plain flour
2 pints/1 liter milk
2 ripe avocados
2 cloves garlic, crushed
3 tablespoons lemon juice
1 tablespoon chopped fresh dill
1/2 cup/100ml heavy/double cream
2 egg yolks
salt and freshly ground black pepper

Fry the onion in the margarine until golden brown. Reduce the heat and sift in the flour. Add the milk, stirring all the time, then bring to the boil and simmer gently until the mixture thickens.

Peel and mash one of the avocados with the garlic and 2 tablespoons of the lemon juice. Peel and cube the other avocado and sprinkle with the remaining lemon juice so that it does not turn black. Over a low heat, stir the mashed avocado into the thickened milk, then add the avocado cubes and dill. Blend the cream and egg yolks together and add them to the soup, with salt and pepper to taste. Serve warm. Serves 6.

Note: Do not allow this soup to boil or the avocado will taste bitter.

MOUSHT IN MANGO SAUCE

St. Peter's fish with puréed mango

juice of 1 lemon
2 tablespoons Worcestershire sauce
salt and freshly ground black pepper
*2 fresh mousht (or trout), about 1 1/4 lb/600g
each, cut into fillets*
2 tablespoons all-purpose/plain flour
vegetable oil
1/4 cup/60g butter
1/2 cup/100ml dry white wine
1 mango

Mix together the lemon juice, Worcestershire sauce, salt and pepper, and pour it over the fish. Allow the fish to marinate for at least 30 minutes. Pour off the marinade and reserve it.

Flour the fish, then pan-fry them in hot oil on both sides. Remove the fish from the pan, discard the oil, and add the butter, white wine, and the reserved marinade juices.

Peel the mango and cut away the flesh. Purée half and thinly slice the rest. Add the slices to the pan. Return the fish to the pan and continue cooking until it flakes easily. Lay the fish on a hot dish. Stir the puréed mango into the pan juices and spoon over the fish. Serves 4.

URI GUTTMANN

◆ *Avocado*

soup.

URI GUTTMANN

◆ *Uri Guttmann is a*

well established

chef who represents

Israel at

congresses and

international

food shows.

He is the owner

of the Panorama

Restaurant in

Tel Aviv.

BANANAS TEL-KATZIR

FILLING
1 cup/225ml milk
1 tablespoon sugar
2 tablespoons butter
vanilla extract/essence
1 tablespoon cornstarch/cornflour
1 egg yolk
salt
3/4 cup/150g shelled pecans
8 fresh dates, pitted and whole
4 dried dates, finely chopped
grated rind of 1 orange

4 bananas, peeled and whole
4 crêpes (thin pancakes)

SAUCE
1/4 cup/60g butter
1 cup/225g sugar
1/2 cup/100ml fresh orange juice

Boil the milk with the sugar, butter and vanilla. Mix the cornstarch with the egg yolk, add a pinch of salt, and add to the boiling milk, stirring well as the mixture thickens. Allow to cool, then cover and chill.

Grind the pecans in a food processor, then add them, with the fresh dates and the finely chopped dried dates, to the chilled custard. Stir in the grated orange rind. Preheat the oven to 425°F/ 220°C.

Put a spoonful of filling and a banana onto each crêpe and roll up. Place in a lightly oiled baking dish, and cook in the oven for about 20 minutes, or until the bananas are soft. Transfer the filled crêpes to a warm serving dish.

To make the sauce, melt the butter in a small saucepan over a very low heat and add the sugar. When the sugar has dissolved, add the orange juice. When the mixture is thoroughly hot, pour it over the crêpes.
Serves 4.

BREAST OF MOULLARD WITH HYSSOP

1 teaspoon honey
2 cloves garlic, finely chopped
2 teaspoons hyssop
salt and freshly ground black pepper
4 tablespoons brandy
1 cup/225ml water
2 tablespoons butter
2 moullard (or duck) breasts,
about 12 oz/350g each
fresh melissa/lemon balm leaves,
to garnish

Mix together the honey, garlic, hyssop, salt and pepper, brandy, and water to make a marinade. Add the moullard breasts and marinate for 2 hours.

Having removed the breasts from the marinade, fry them quickly in butter on both sides, transfer them to a baking dish, add half the marinade, and cook for 5 minutes on each side in a hot oven. Slice the breasts, and serve sprinkled with hyssop, with the marinade as a sauce. Garnish with melissa leaves. Serves 4.

EREZ KOMAROVSKY

LAMB CUTLETS WITH WATERMELON

12 lamb cutlets
1/2 cup/100ml red wine
1/4 cup/60ml extra-virgin olive oil
1 clove garlic, thinly sliced
4 tablespoons finely chopped fresh coriander
sprig lemon grass (Cymbopogon citratus), minced very fine
sprig fresh sorrel
sprig salad rocket
1 lb/450g watermelon, without skin or seeds
8 oz/225g goat's cheese

Marinate the lamb cutlets in the wine, olive oil, garlic, coriander and lemon grass for 1 hour. Wash the sorrel and salad rocket and pat dry. Cut the watermelon into small regular-sized strips.

Put the cutlets in the broiler/grill pan with a little of the marinade, and cook under a hot broiler/grill for a few minutes. Turn the cutlets and put a slice of goat's cheese on each. Cook for another 5 minutes or so until the cutlets are done, but don't overcook them. Serve the cutlets on a bed of sorrel, salad rocket and watermelon strips, with some of the grilling juices poured over them.

Serves 6.

FIGS AND PRICKLY PEARS WITH ROSE & VANILLA YOGURT

1/2 cup/100g sugar
1/2 cup/100ml water
1/2 vanilla pod
handful of rose petals
1 cup/225ml plain fresh yogurt
butter
1 lb/450g ripe figs
1 lb/450g prickly pears

Dissolve the sugar in the water, then add the vanilla pod and most of the rose petals. Bring to a boil and simmer for 5 minutes. Pour the liquid through a nylon sieve and let it cool. Now stir the yogurt into it and put the mixture in the refrigerator for at least 1 hour. Pre-heat the oven to 390°F/ 200°C.

Wash and dry the figs. Carefully peel the prickly pears, under running water, preferably with gloves on, and place them on a buttered baking sheet. Bake for 10 minutes. Serve hot with the cold sauce, decorated with the rest of the rose petals.

Serves 6 to 8.

◆ *Erez Komarovsky offers Japanese delicacies with an Israeli flavor.*

EREZ
KOMAROVSKY

RED SNAPPER WITH MYRTLE

1 extremely fresh red snapper,
weighing 2lbs/900g
6 cups/1.2 liters water
1 tablespoon sea salt
fresh myrtle leaves
1/2 cup/100 ml extra-virgin olive oil
1 chili pepper, very finely chopped
4 cloves garlic, crushed
4 baby eggplants/aubergines
2 or 3 lemons

Fillet the fish and make several diagonal incisions in the skin. Bring the water and salt to a boil. Plunge the fillets into the boiling water for 30 seconds, then transfer them immediately to a bowl of ice-cold water. When cold, drain and pat dry with paper towels/kitchen paper.

Rub the myrtle leaves between your hands to release their fragrance and put them in a shallow dish with the chili (wear gloves while you are chopping it!) and garlic. Lay the fillets in the dish. Steam the eggplants until soft, remove the skins and put them in the dish as well.

Allow the fillets to marinate for at least 3 hours, turning once so that they absorb the other flavors.

When ready to serve, remove the fillets from the marinade, drain them and garnish with one of the eggplants cut into quarters.

Serves 4 as a main course or 8 as a starter.

◆*A*

version

of red

snapper

with

myrtle.

RED MULLET IN GRAPE LEAVES

8 large fresh grape/vine leaves
4 tablespoons olive oil
juice of 1 lemon
1 tablespoon chopped fresh parsley
20 coriander seeds
1 tablespoon fresh chopped basil
salt and freshly ground black pepper
8 red mullet, about 8oz/225g each,
cleaned and patted dry

Blanch the grape leaves in hot water for 20 seconds, then drain on paper towels/kitchen paper (if you are using grape leaves preserved in brine, see instructions given for stuffed grape leaves, p. 28). Mix together the olive oil, lemon juice, parsley, coriander seeds, basil, salt and pepper. Prick the fish all over with a needle, spread the oil and herb mixture over them and leave them to marinate for 1 hour.

Fold a grape leaf around each fish, leaving the head sticking out. Brush the leaves with olive oil. Pre-heat the broiler or grill and cook for 2 minutes on each side. Serve with other *mezze*. Serves 8.

BOTTLED KUMQUATS

2 lb/450g fresh kumquats
1 1/2 cups/350ml water
4 cups/450g sugar
1 tablespoon rose water, if liked

Wash the kumquats thoroughly, then slice them lengthwise. In a large saucepan, dissolve the sugar in the water, add the kumquats, bring to a boil, and simmer gently for 1 hour. Remove from the heat, stir in the rosewater, and allow to cool. Store in a jar with a tightly fitting lid.

MEDITERRANEAN TART

PASTRY
2 cups/225g all-purpose/plain flour
1 cup/225ml olive oil
1/3 cup/80ml water
1 egg
salt and freshly ground black pepper

FILLING
1 small eggplant/aubergine
2 cloves garlic, finely chopped
2 onions, thinly sliced
1/4 cup/60ml olive oil
6 small tomatoes, thinly sliced
4 small zucchini/courgettes, thinly sliced
1 teaspoon fresh thyme
2/3 cup/150g black olives, pitted and halved
salt and freshly ground black pepper

Put all the pastry ingredients in a food processor and mix for 2 minutes with a plastic blade. Roll the dough into a ball, wrap it in plastic wrap/cling film, and chill in the refrigerator for 1 hour.

Cut the eggplant/aubergine in half lengthwise and slice each half very thinly. Using a moderate heat, fry the garlic, onions and eggplant in the olive oil for about 15 minutes, or until the eggplant softens. Stir in the salt, pepper and most of the thyme, and set aside. Pre-heat the oven to 425°F/220°C.

Roll out the pastry and line a tart pan (the type with a removable base). Cut off any excess pastry around the edges, and prick the base with a fork. Spread the eggplant and onion mixture over the pastry, and arrange the tomatoes and zucchini decoratively on top. Top with the olives, add a sprinkling of thyme, and brush with olive oil. Bake for 45 minutes. Serve hot or cold.

Serves 5 or 6.

ISRAEL AHARONI

◆ *Israel Aharoni,*

owner and chef

of one of

Israel's leading

Chinese

restaurants,

Yin-Yang.

Aharoni's other

passion is

French food.

◆ *Mediterrenean*

tart.

ZACHI BUKSHESTER

◆ *Zachi*

Bukshester

is the owner

and chef of

The Pink

Ladle. He

serves Israeli

nouvelle

cuisine with

great

attention to

presentation.

HORN OF PLENTY

4 leaves filo *pastry*
1 tablespoon flour
vegetable oil

MARINADE
1 tablespoon olive oil
1/2 tablespoon brown sugar
1 tablespoon white wine vinegar
1 clove garlic

BEAN SAUCE
1 lb/450g fresh fava/broad beans
1/4 cup/60ml cream
1 cup/225ml chicken broth/stock
dill, nutmeg, salt and pepper to taste

FILLING
1/2 lb/225g fillet steak, cubed
1/2 lb/225g fillet of sea bass
1 tablespoon pistachio nuts, shelled
1 small onion, chopped
2 oz/60g carrots, diced small
2 oz/60g leeks, chopped
6 oz/180g asparagus, chopped
2 oz/60g turnips, diced small
1/2 cup/100ml dry red wine

Roll each leaf of *filo* into a cone shape, sticking the pastry to itself with a dab of flour and water. Allow the cones to dry.

Mix the marinade ingredients together, add the beef, fish, pistachios and onion, and allow to marinate for 1 hour.

Boil or steam the beans until just tender, then drain. Purée them with the cream, chicken broth and spices in the food processor, and keep warm.

Simmer or steam the carrots, leeks, asparagus and turnips until they are *al dente*.

Drain the beef, fish, pistachios and onion, sauté them in butter in a hot skillet/frying pan, and add the cooked vegetables and red wine.

Deep fry the *filo* cones until they are crisp and golden, then fill them with the meat and vegetable mixture. Make sure the bean purée is nice and hot, then spoon it onto individual plates and place a filled *filo* cone on top.
Serves 4.

PRICKLY PEARS FLAMBÉES

1/2 tablespoon butter
1 teaspoon brown sugar
powdered cardamom
2 prickly pears per person, peeled and sliced
2 tablespooons Sabra or Grand Marnier liqueur
whipped cream, to serve

Melt half the butter, add the sugar and cardamom powder, and sauté the prickly pear slices in this mixture for 1/2 minute. Add the liqueur and set light to it. When the flames die down, add the remaining butter and allow it to melt. Serve with whipped cream.

FRIED GOAT'S CHEESE WITH MINT SALAD
See p. 56

◆ *Horn of*

plenty

ITAMAR DAVIDOV

◆ *Itamar*

Davidov is

chef and owner

of the Pitango

restaurant.

He blends

local produce

with French

tradition and

is renowned

for his food

combinations.

JERUSALEM ARTICHOKE CREAM SOUP

1 lb/450g Jerusalem artichokes, peeled
2 pints/1 liter chicken broth/stock
juice of 1 lemon
4 oz/100g chicken breast, skinned and cubed
1/4 cup/60g butter
3 tablespoons all-purpose/plain flour
salt and freshly ground white pepper
4 strands saffron
1 cup/225ml heavy/double cream
freshly ground black pepper

Cook the artichokes in the chicken broth and lemon juice until they begin to soften. Strain off the broth and reserve it, then purée the artichokes, adding just enough broth to make blending easy.

Stir-fry the chicken cubes in half the butter - 2 minutes is enough, or until the pink turns white. Drain on paper towels/ kitchen paper.

Melt the remaining butter, add the flour and cook for 3 or 4 minutes, stirring constantly. Stir in the reserved chicken broth, artichoke purée, salt, white pepper and saffron. Bring slowly to a boil, stirring all the time, and allow to simmer for 5 minutes.

Add the chicken cubes and adjust the seasoning if necessary. At the last minute, stir in the cream. Serve sprinkled with black pepper. Serves 5 or 6.

DATES & POPPY SEEDS IN HOT TOFFEE

1/2 cup/100ml heavy/double cream
1/2 cup/100g sugar
2 tablespoons water
20 fresh dates, pitted and whole
3 teaspoons fried poppy seeds
1 1/2 cups/350ml heavy/double cream, whipped

Heat the 1/2 cup/100ml cream in a bain-marie. In a small saucepan, dissolve the sugar in the water, turn up the heat and boil until the mixture turns golden. Remove from the heat and stir in the hot cream. Bring the mixture to the boil and cook for 5 minutes, stirring all the time. The mixture should now be toffee, thick and smooth. Stir in the dates and poppy seeds and cook for another minute or two. Serve warm, topped with the whipped cream.

Serves 4.

◆ *Dates*

and

poppy

seeds in

hot toffee.

CELIA REGEV & REVIVA APPEL

◆ *Celia and*

Reviva are

restaurateurs

who have

introduced

new tastes in

pastries and

desserts.

JAFFAS BAVAROISE

6 oranges
fresh mint or citrus leaves, to garnish

BAVARIAN CREAM FILLING
1/2 cup/100g sugar
8 egg yolks
1 cup/225ml orange juice
2 level teaspoons/10ml gelatin
1 cup/225g heavy/double cream, whipped

SAUCE
1/2 cup/100g sugar
1 cup/225ml orange juice
4 tablespoons lemon juice

Peel the oranges and remove the segments. Grease 6 individual molds with butter and line the bottom of each with a circle of wax/greaseproof paper cut to size. Sprinkle the sides of the molds with sugar and tap out the excess. Line the sides of the molds with orange segments, trimming them to fit snugly.

To make the Bavarian cream filling, whip/whisk the egg yolks and sugar together until pale and fluffy, then bring the orange juice to a boil and add it to the egg yolks. Dissolve the gelatin according to the instructions on the packet. Cook the egg yolks and orange juice over a low heat until the mixture is thick enough to coat the back of a wooden spoon, then add the dissolved gelatin. Stir well and pass through a sieve. Allow the mixture to cool, then put it in the refrigerator until it is on the point of setting.

Remove from the refrigerator and fold in the whipped cream. Pour the cream into the molds and leave to set for 3 or 4 hours.

To make the sauce, dissolve the sugar in the orange and lemon juice, bring to a boil, and simmer for a few minutes to thicken. When cool, spoon onto individual plates and turn out the molds. Decorate with a mint or citrus leaf. Serves 6.

SORBET OGEN

1 1/4 cups/300g sugar
1 1/4 cups/300ml water
11 oz/300g puréed Ogen melon, chilled
juice of 1 lemon

Dissolve the sugar in the water and bring to a boil. As soon as the mixture begins to bubble, remove from the heat, cool, then refrigerate.

Mix the puréed melon with the lemon juice and the chilled syrup, pour into a shallow container and put in the icebox/freezer until barely firm. Remove from the freezer and blend to a smooth consistency, then re-freeze. Serve in chilled glasses with sugar-frosted rims. Serves 4.

◆ *Jaffa*

bavaroise.

DALIA PENN-LERNER

SALAD OF FOIE GRAS & POMEGRANATE

8 oz/225g fresh foie gras (or chicken livers)
various salad leaves (romaine/cos, radiccio,
endive, spinach)
1 tablespoon white wine vinegar
2 or 3 tablespoons pomegranate seeds
salt and freshly ground black pepper

DRESSING
1 tablespoon white wine vinegar
1 tablespoon lemon juice
4 tablespoons olive oil
salt and pepper

Cut the liver into 1/2-inch/1-cm cubes. Cover and refrigerate until firm. Put the salad leaves in a bowl, beat together the dressing ingredients, pour over the salad and toss well.

Pre-heat a non-stick skillet/frying pan (only add oil if you are using chicken livers, which have very little fat compared to goose liver). Quickly stir-fry the liver - the cubes should remain pink inside - and transfer to a warm plate.

Pour off any fat that has accumulated in the skillet, and add the vinegar. Remove from the heat, return the liver cubes to the skillet and season with salt and pepper. Spoon the warm liver and the pomegranate seeds over the salad and serve immediately. Serves 4.

CHEESE PARCELS

full fat feta or goat's cheese
fresh savory or thyme, finely chopped
filo pastry
melted butter
fruit (watermelon, ripe figs, grapes)

Mash the cheese with a fork and season with savory or thyme. Cut the sheets of *filo* into 4-inch/10-cm squares. Place a teaspoon of the cheese mixture in the center of each and draw the sides up to form a little pouch. Press the edges together with water to seal them. Pre-heat the oven to 375°F/190°C.

Brush the pouches with melted butter and bake for 10-15 minutes until crisp and golden. Serve with cubes of watermelon, figs, grapes, etc.

If making pouches sounds too fiddly, you could make triangular or square parcels instead. Deep-frying would also be an alternative to baking.

◆ *Dalia Penn-Lerner, a former actress, is a chef, food writer and editor who has travelled widely.*

◆ *Cheese parcels.*

236

$\mathcal{I}$ N D E X

Recipes and their page numbers are given in bold; page numbers in roman type refer to pictures.